The Medieval World
Activity Support Guide

Simon Rodden • Norman Hobson • Bea Stimpson

Stanley Thornes (Publishers) Ltd

Applications for such permissions should be addressed to the publishers: Stanley Thornes (Publishers) Ltd, Ellenborough House, Wellington Street, CHELTENHAM GL50 IYW, England.

First published in 1998 by:
Stanley Thornes (Publishers) Ltd
Ellenborough House
Wellington Street
CHELTENHAM GL50 IYW
England

98 99 00 01 02 / 10 9 8 7 6 5 4 3 2 1

A catalogue record for this book is available from the British Library.

ISBN 0-7487-3586-0

Page layout by Janet McCallum
Illustrated by Francis Bacon, Steve Ballinger, Beverly Curl and Angela Lumley
Cover artwork by Beverly Curl
Printed and bound in Great Britain by Ashford Colour Press, Gosport, Hampshire

Contents

Introduction   5
Key Elements matching guide   6
Sample level descriptors mark sheet   7
Level descriptors mark sheet   8
Self assessment sheet   9

Chapter numbers correspond to those in the pupils' book.

1 The Norman invasion

A Basic skills: Vowels   10
B Quick quiz   11
C True or false   12
D Norman shields   13
E Edgar, the housecarl   14
F The Battle of Hastings   15
G Extension activity   16

The Bayeux Tapestry
A Basic skills: Syllables   17
B Quick quiz   18
C Scenes from the Tapestry   19
D Extension activity   20

2 Control of the English

Castles
A Basic skills: Question marks and
   exclamation marks   21
B Quick quiz   22
C Motte and bailey castles   23
D Siege!   24
E Castle development   25
F Extension activity   26

The feudal system
A Basic skills: Masculine and
   feminine nouns   27
B Quick quiz   28
C Heads and tails   29
D Schools and feudal systems   30
E Advantages and disadvantages   32
F A monk's account   33
G Extension activity   34

The Domesday Book
A Basic skills: Abbreviations   35
B Quick quiz   36
C Questions and answers   37
D Kent, the first entry   38
E Villages   39
F Words and abbreviations   40
G Extension activity   41

3 Village life

A Basic skills: Capital letters   42
B Quick quiz   43
C Surnames   44
D Sorting names   45
E Living in a cottage   46
F Sickness   47
G Extension activity   48

4 The farming year

A Basic skills: Collective nouns   49
B Quick quiz   50
C Working on the farm   51
D The farming calendar   52
E Disasters   54
F Extension activity   55

5 Pastimes and sports

A Basic skills: Consonants   56
B Quick quiz   57
C Football and cock-fighting   58
D Extension activity   59

6 Crime and punishment

A Basic skills: Doubles   60
B Quick quiz   61
C Punishment   62
D A public execution   63
E Trials   64
F Extension activity   65

7 Religion

A Basic skills: Key words   66
B Quick quiz   67
C Church architecture   68
D Monastery services   69
E Monks' winter timeline   70
F You could become a monk!   71
G Festivals and processions   73
H Joining the Church   76
I Monastery jobs   77
J Chaucer and the Church   78
K Extension activity   79

Becket and pilgrims
A Basic skills: Commas   80
B Quick quiz   81
C True or false   82
D Becket's life   83
E The murder of Becket   84
F Dilemmas   85

Contents *continued*

G Can you stop Becket's murder? 86
H Picturing the murder 87
I An eyewitness account 88
J Why was Becket killed? 89
K Pilgrims and pilgrimages 91
L The Canterbury Tales 92
M Visiting a shrine 94
N Extension activity 95

8 The Crusades

A Basic skills: Capital letters, commas and full stops 96
B Quick quiz 97
C Labels 98
D The First Crusade Part 2 99
E Effects of the Crusades 100
F Extension activity 101

9 Inventions

A Basic skills: Compound words 102
B Quick quiz 103
C When were they invented? 104
D Which treatment? 105
E Medicine 106
F Extension activity 107

10 The Magna Carta

A Basic skills: Prefixes 108
B Quick quiz 109
C Why was King John unpopular? 110
D 'Trouble with the Church' 111
E Magna Carta extracts 112
F Extension activity 113

11 The growth of Parliament

A Basic skills: Using a dictionary 115
B Quick quiz 116
C How did Parliament develop? 117
D Extension activity 118

12 Wales and Scotland

A Basic skills: Nationalities 119
B Quick quiz 120
C Beaumaris Castle 121
D United kingdoms? 122
E Scottish history 123
F Extension activity 124

13 The Black Death

A Basic skills: Colour words 125
B Quick quiz 126
C Concoct a cure 127
D A bishop's account 128
E Symptoms 129
F A monk's description 130
G Extension activity 131

14 The Peasants' Revolt

A Basic skills: Possessive apostrophes 133
B Quick quiz 134
C Pictures of the Revolt 135
D Historical chain 137
E A law case 138
F Extension activity 139

15 Language in medieval times

(No worksheets for this topic.)

16 Town life

A Basic skills: Nouns 140
B Quick quiz 141
C Merchant guilds 142
D Imports and exports 143
E Guilds and apprentices 144
F Extension activity 145

17 The 100 Years' War

A Basic skills: Homophones 146
B Quick quiz 147
C The longbow 148
D The Battle of Agincourt 149
E War grid 150
F Extension activity 152

18 The Wars of the Roses

A Basic skills: Sentences 153
B Quick quiz 154
C Timeline 155
D A family extract 156
E Extension activity 157

19 Kings of England

A Basic skills: Paragraphs 158
B Quick quiz 159
C Extension activity 160

The worksheets in this *Activity Support Guide* have been designed to give pupils experience in working on a range of activities which incorporate the five Key Elements of Study Unit 1: Medieval Realms, as required by the National Curriculum History document. The worksheets, based on the content of the pupils' book, revise and reinforce the Key Elements covered in each topic.

Pupils work through carefully differentiated worksheets ranging from simple, highly structured activities to more demanding extended writing tasks where the emphasis is on differentiation by outcome.

Depending on the learning needs of pupils, all or a selection of worksheets from each topic may be chosen. Each topic allows pupils to develop skills in several of the Key Elements.

Pupils are encouraged to keep a portfolio of completed work and to fill in their own assessment sheets (see page 9).

A feature of this *Activity Support Guide* is the inclusion of a Basic Skills worksheet for each topic. This highlights word origins, common grammar and punctuation teaching points and gives pupils practice in becoming aware of the importance of correct presentation in their work.

As pupils complete the range of worksheets for each topic, the teacher, using the marking criteria guide for the level descriptors, can decide on a National Curriculum working level for each pupil.

By the end of the Study Unit, both teachers and pupils will have built up an accumulative record of achievement based on enjoyable and vigorous learning.

Topic	Key Elements covered				
1 **The Norman invasion** The Bayeux Tapestry	1a	2 b d 2 b	3a	4ab	5abc 5a c
2 **Control of the English** Castles The feudal system The Domesday Book	1a 1 b 1 b	2ab 2ab d 2a		4a 4a 4ab	5abc 5abc 5abc
3 **Village life**		2ab		4ab	5abc
4 **The farming year**		2ab		4a	5abc
5 **Pastimes and sports**		2a		4a	5 bc
6 **Crime and punishment**		2ab		4ab	5abc
7 **Religion** Becket and pilgrims	1 b 1a	2a c 2abc		4a 4ab	5abc 5abc
8 **The Crusades**	1ab	2 bc			5abc
9 **Inventions**		2a d			5 bc
10 **The Magna Carta**	1ab	2ab c	3ab	4ab	5abc
11 **The growth of Parliament**	1a	2ab	3ab	4ab	5abc
12 **Wales and Scotland**	1a	2abcd			5abc
13 **The Black Death**	1 b	2ab d	3a	4ab	5abc
14 **The Peasants' Revolt**	1a	2ab d	3ab	4ab	5abc
16 **Town life**		2ab		4ab	5abc
17 **The 100 Years' War**	1ab	2ab d		4ab	5abc
18 **The Wars of the Roses**	1ab	2ab	3ab	4ab	5a c
19 **Kings of England**	1a	2ab d		4a	5abc

Sample level descriptors mark sheet

Study Unit 1: Medieval Realms

Topic | Becket and pilgrims

Key Elements covered	1	2	3	4	5
	a	abc		ab	abc

Level descriptors
A Almost faultless
B High degree of accuracy
C Balance of understanding with some errors
D Experienced difficulty
E Significant difficulties/no evidence

WORKSHEETS

NAME	A	B	C	D	E	F	G	H	I	J	K	L	M	N	O	NC working level
J Bloggs	B	B	C	A	B	B	C	B	B	B	A	B	C	B	C	5

Study Unit 1: Medieval Realms

Topic

Key Elements covered	1	2	3	4	5

Level descriptors
A   Almost faultless
B   High degree of accuracy
C   Balance of understanding with some errors
D   Experienced difficulty
E   Significant difficulties/no evidence

WORKSHEETS

NAME	A	B	C	D	E	F	G	H	I	J	K	L	M	N	O	NC working level

Self assessment sheet

Time line

Name _____

Date _____

Topic _____

I learnt about _____

I put the following pieces of work in my folder:

_____

_____

_____

The most interesting part of the topic was _____

_____

_____

_____

_____

_____

It was the most interesting part because _____

_____

_____

_____

_____

_____

_____

A Basic skills: Vowels

Look at page 7 in your textbook.

Fill in the missing vowels to finish this picture of a Norman knight.

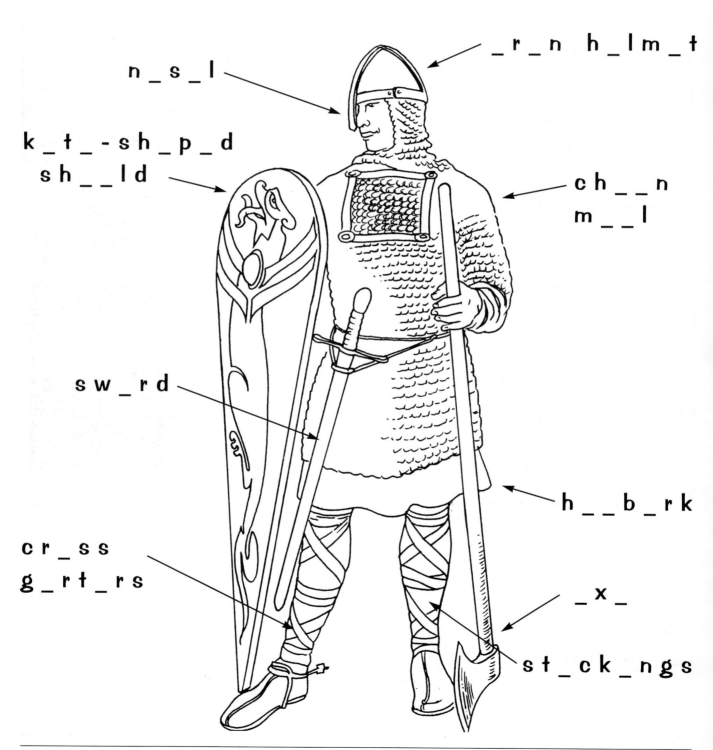

n _ s _ l

_ r _ n   h _ l m _ t

k _ t _ - s h _ p _ d
s h _ _ l d

c h _ _ n
m _ _ l

s w _ r d

h _ _ b _ r k

c r _ s s
g _ r t _ r s

_ x _

s t _ c k _ n g s

B Quick quiz

Look at page 5 in your textbook.

1   Write these labels on the map on the right:

Normandy

Norway

England

2   Write these battle sites on the map below:

Battle of Hastings

Battle of Stamford Bridge

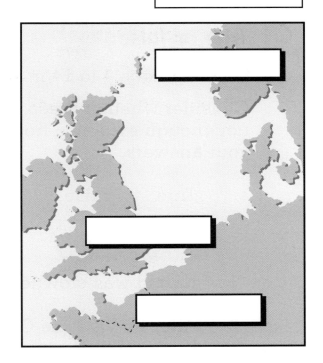

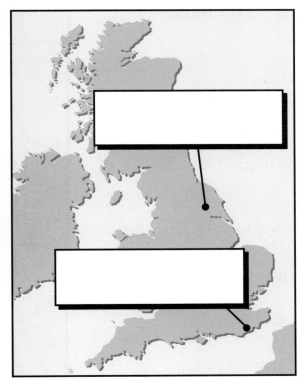

3 a Who is this?

_____

b Which country was he king of?

_____

4 a What is this? _____

b Did people believe it would bring good luck or bad luck?

_____

C *True or false*

Look at pages 4 to 14 in your textbook.

Consider whether these statements are true or false, or if there is not enough evidence from the text to decide. Fill in the boxes with your answers.

True	False	Not enough evidence
✓	✗	?

1   Harold was crowned King of England in 1966.

2   After Edward the Confessor died, his son was made King of England.

3   King Hardrada attacked William at the Battle of Stamford Bridge.

4   William attacked Harold at Hastings.

5   William's knights were unshaven.

6   Harold had two brothers to help him at the Battle of Hastings.

7   William's army travelled in helicopters to England.

8   William brought lots of his relatives to England.

9   Harold's army were called housemaids.

10   Harold was scared of William.

11   William was crowned King of England in 1066.

12   At the time of the Battle of Hastings, all the armour was made from leather.

You will need

D Norman shields

Look at page 7 in your textbook.

1 Look at these pictures of Norman shields.

2 Practise designing your own shields.

3 Choose your best design and draw it here. Colour in your picture of a Norman knight.

E | *Edgar, the housecarl*

Look at page 8 in your textbook.

Imagine you are one of Harold's housecarls.

Help words and ideas

frightened   unhappy   scared

it is my duty

worried about my family

Harold is our King

I am fighting to protect my country

I have got mixed feelings

we are in a good defensive position

My name is Edgar. I am one of King Harold's housecarls. We are the best soldiers in Harold's army. Tomorrow we may fight against William. This is how I feel tonight.

_____

_____

_____

_____

_____

_____

_____

_____

_____

_____

_____

You will need

F *The Battle of Hastings*

Look at pages 10 to 12 in your textbook.

What happened at these times during the battle? Draw a picture and write a sentence here to show what was happening.

Dawn		
9.30am		
Midday		
4.00pm		
Dusk		
Night		

G *Extension activity*

Answer questions 2 to 6 in sentences.

1 Which three leaders wanted to be the next King of England when Edward the Confessor died?

  1 _____

  2 _____

  3 _____

2 Choose one of the three and say why he wanted to be the next King.

3 King Hardrada attacked England first. Where did the battle between him and Harold take place?

4 Harold's soldiers camped at Senlac Hill. Why did he choose this site for the battle?

5 What trick helped the Normans to win the Battle of Hastings?

6 What do you think would have happened if William and Hardrada had attacked England at the same time?

A *Basic skills: Syllables*

Divide these words into syllables to help your spelling. Remember that all syllables must include a vowel: a, e, i, o, u. In some words, like 'navy', 'tapestry', and 'dying', the 'y' is classed as a vowel. One word has been done for you.

throne   Senlac Hill

Bayeux ~~Tapestry~~   army

defensive   William the Conqueror

Normandy

Battle of Hastings

knights   Duke

Harold

invaded

One syllable words	Two syllable words	Three syllable words
		Tap-es-try

You will need

B **Quick quiz**

Look at pages 5 to 13 in your textbook.

<u>Underline</u> the correct answer from the words or phrases in brackets.

1 What country is Bayeux in? (England, France, Norway)

2 The Tapestry is made of (linen, plastic, wood).

3 The Tapestry tells the story of the Battle of
   (Britain, Hastings, Stamford Bridge).

4 The writing on the Tapestry is in (French, English, Latin).

5 The Tapestry is made up of (62, 72, 82) strips.

6 By what name is this comet known today? _____

7 The comet was thought to be a sign from whom? _____

8 The comet has never been seen since 1066 (true, false).

9 Whose ship is this? _____

10 What clue is there on the ship that tells you whose ship it is?

_____

C Scenes from the Tapestry

Look at pages 4 to 13 in your textbook.

Cut out and put these pictures into the correct order. When you have done that, write a few sentences explaining what is happening in each scene.

You will need

D Extension activity

1 Is the Bayeux Tapestry an important historical record? Give reasons for your answer.

2 Do you think the Bayeux Tapestry is biased in its account? Give reasons for your answer.

3 Why was the Tapestry made? Wouldn't it have been simpler and quicker to write an account of William conquering England, rather than using pictures?

4 Imagine the English had been asked to contribute to the making of the Tapestry. How might they have shown how they were treated by the Normans? You could draw your response in the boxes below.

You will need

A Basic skills: Question marks and exclamation marks

Look at pages 16 and 17 in your textbook.

A question mark (?) is used at the end of a sentence which asks a question, for example, 'How far is it to Rochester Castle?' It is used instead of a full stop. The next word after a question mark begins with a capital letter.

An exclamation mark (!) is used at the end of a sentence or phrase to highlight some special meaning. For example, 'Help, we are being attacked!'

Use either an exclamation mark / **!** / or a question mark / **?** / to complete these sentences or phrases.

1 a How can we break through the castle walls

   b Should we attack the castle using the siege tower

   c We shall not surrender

   d When was the Tower of London built

   e Did the soldiers in Rochester Castle surrender

   f I have been shot in the leg

   g Why were motte and bailey castles built

   h Stop them, they are coming over the wall

2 Look at pages 15 to 19. Write down five questions you could ask a friend about castles and seiges.

3 Write down five sentences or phrases that need an exclamation mark.

You will need

B Quick quiz

Look at pages 15 to 19 in your textbook.

1   Find the matching pairs from these words. Draw lines to join the right words together. One has been done for you.

curtain   Castle

square   bailey

Rochester   keep

concentric   keep

motte   castle

court   walls

stone   yard

roundshell   tower

2   Write the number of these castles in the circle next to their correct locations on the map. Use an atlas to help you.

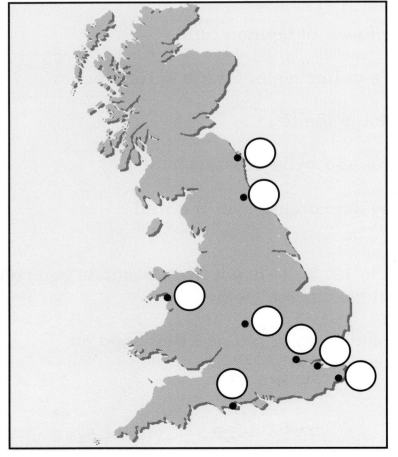

① Bamburgh Castle

② Corfe Castle

③ Dover Castle

④ Durham Castle

⑤ Harlech Castle

⑥ Rochester Castle

⑦ Tower of London

⑧ Warwick Castle

C Motte and bailey castles

Look at page 15 in your textbook.

This is a motte and bailey castle. Write the labels below in the correct places.

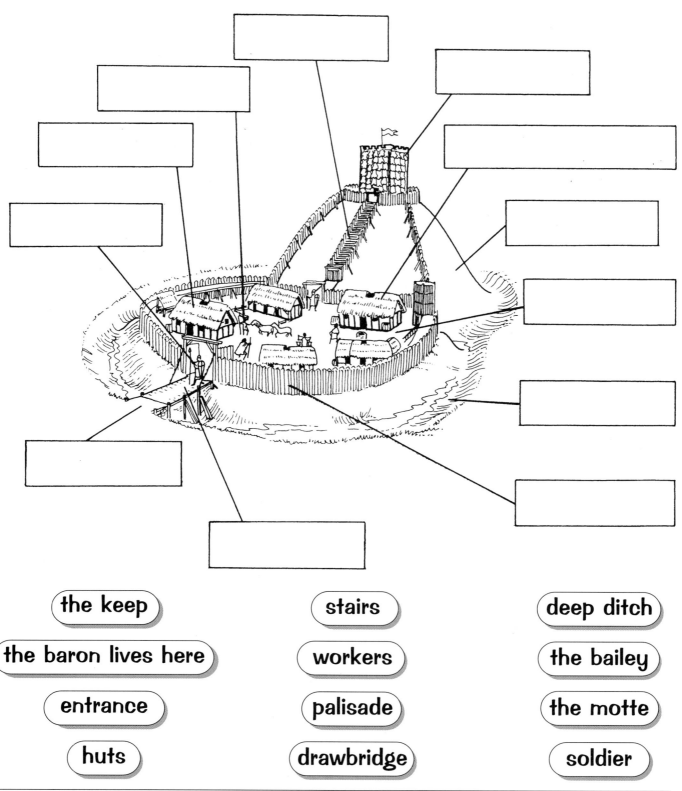

the keep   stairs   deep ditch

the baron lives here   workers   the bailey

entrance   palisade   the motte

huts   drawbridge   soldier

D Siege!

Look at pages 16 to 18 in your textbook.

How can I capture this castle?

How can I defend my castle?

I shall attack the castle using the trebouchet. It works by

_____

_____

_____

They are using a trebouchet. I can defend my castle from this weapon by

_____

_____

_____

I shall use my siege tower. It is a good weapon to attack a castle with because

_____

_____

_____

They are using a siege tower to attack the castle. I can defend the castle against this weapon by

_____

_____

_____

I shall mine the castle walls. Mining works this way

_____

_____

_____

They are mining the castle walls. I can defend the castle against mining by

_____

_____

_____

We have been unable to break into the castle. I shall have to lay siege to it. Laying siege to a castle means

_____

_____

They are laying siege to the castle. What will happen to us?

_____

_____

E | Castle development

Look at pages 15 to 19 in your textbook.

1   Cut out and place these pictures of castles in order of their
    development. Start with the simplest design.

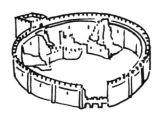

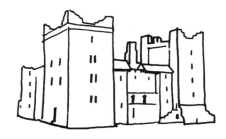

2   What changes do you notice between these castles? The
    following words may help you.
    • **Materials**: What were they built from? Why did the materials
      change?
    • **Shape**: Why did the shape change?
    • **Size**: Did they remain the same size?
    • **Site** (location): Was their location important? Why?

3   Did castles remain important military strongholds for very
    long?

4   Why did castles change from being strongholds to being
    stately homes?

F *Extension activity*

Use the information on page 16 to answer these questions.

1 Explain in your own words why King John decided to mine the walls of Rochester Castle.

2 Describe how the miners prepared to mine the castle walls.

3 What happened to the walls that were mined?

4 How could Rochester Castle have been defended against mining?

5 Using a dictionary, write down what these words mean:

   a fortress   _____

   b garrison   _____

   c siege   _____

   d barricade   _____

   e starvation   _____

   f surrender   _____

6 Using a thesaurus, find a word or words that means the same as the words below:

   a fortress   _____

   b garrison   _____

   c siege   _____

   d barricade   _____

   e starvation   _____

   f surrender   _____

A Basic skills: Masculine and feminine nouns

'Lord' is masculine. 'Lady' is feminine. What are the missing masculine and feminine nouns in the following lists? The first one has been done for you.

Masculine	Feminine
lord	lady
	abbess
baron	
bachelor	
	countess
heir	
	marchioness
mayor	
prince	
	nun
hero	
	female
king	
shepherd	
	duck
	sow
	widow
peacock	
	ewe
stag	
manservant	
	peeress

 Quick quiz

Look at pages 20 to 23 in your textbook.

1 Fill in the missing words.

a This is the _____

He owes allegiance to _____

_____

b These are _____

They owe allegiance to _____

_____

c These are _____

They owe allegiance to _____

_____

d These are _____

They owe allegiance to _____

_____

2 <u>Underline</u> the correct answer from the words or phrases in brackets.

    a Feudal means (land, fighting, money).

    b There were more knights than peasants (true, false).

    c The king owed allegiance to the barons (true, false).

    d Bishops owed allegiance only to God (true, false).

    e Knights took orders only from the king (true, false).

C Heads and tails

Match the heads to the correct tails with a line.

Heads   **Tails**

| 1 William gave land to the barons | with knights for his army. |

| 2 Barons supplied the king | very important. |

| 3 William was Duke of Normandy as | in return for services. |

| 4 Feudal is a word | well as King of England. |

| 5 Owning land was | with money when he requested it. |

| 6 In return for land, the bishops | provided the king with knights for his army. |

| 7 The bishop also | paid homage to the king every year. |

| 8 The bishop threatened with God's anger | prayed for God's help to win battles. |

| 9 In return for land the barons | asked his monks to write important documents in Latin. |

| 10 The barons also | anyone who disobeyed the king. |

| 11 The barons provided the king | that means land. |

You will need

D | Schools and feudal systems

Look at pages 21 to 23 in your textbook.

We are going to look at your school system and the feudal system to see if there are any similarities. Both the feudal system and your school need to be well organised.

First, look at the roles and responsibilities in your school.

Your **headteacher/principal** is Mr/Mrs/Ms _____

He/she is responsible to _____

His/her main responsibilities are _____

_____

Your **senior deputy head(s)** or **vice principals** are

_____

They are responsible to _____

Their main responsibilities are _____

_____

Heads of departments (curriculum)

How many? _____

They are responsible to

_____

Their main responsibilities are

_____

_____

Heads of year (pastoral)

How many? _____

They are responsible to

_____

Their main responsibilities are

_____

_____

Classroom teachers

Are responsible to _____

Are responsible for _____

Pupils

Are responsible to _____

Are responsible for _____

 D *Schools and feudal systems (continued)*

Now look at the roles and responsibilities in the feudal system.

King

Was responsible to _____

His responsibilities were _____

Tenants-in-chief

Barons and earls

Were responsible to

_____

Were responsible for

_____

_____

Archbishops and bishops

Were responsible to

_____

Were responsible for

_____

_____

Knights

Were responsible to

_____

Were responsible for

_____

_____

Priests and monks

Were responsible to

_____

Were responsible for

_____

_____

Peasants

Were responsible to _____

Were responsible for _____

What similarities can you see between the two systems?
Here are some ideas:

**huge responsibility   not often seen   spiritual well-being
power   lot of work for little or no money
little responsibility   looked after   uniforms   no escape!**

You will need

E *Advantages and disadvantages*

Look at pages 20 to 23 in your textbook.

Advantages   **Disadvantages**

> I like the feudal system because it controls everyone. It provides me with an army and helps me to rule the country.

> I do not like the feudal system because I might not trust my tenants-in-chief. I might not be able to control them and their armies might grow too big. I might not like the advice the Church leaders give me.

F A *monk's account*

Look at page 14 in your textbook.

This is what a monk of the time, Ordericus Vitalis, wrote about William after he had crushed a fourth rebellion in the north of England in 1069.

> Never did William commit so much cruelty; to his lasting disgrace... He ordered all the corn and cattle with all the farming tools and every sort of food collected in heaps and set on fire and so destroyed at once everything that could help to support life in the whole country lying beyond the River Humber.

Answer these questions to help understand why William acted as he did.

1 Why did William do these things as well as kill the rebels?

2 Explain why he decided to destroy the farming tools as well as the crops.

3 Reports of the time say that people turned to cannibalism. Why do you think this happened?

4 The effect of William's actions would last much longer than a few months. Can you think of three reasons why?

You will need
Dictionary

G *Extension activity*

1 Complete these paragraphs.

   a The feudal system could not have worked without peasant labour because of the following reasons.

   b The feudal system could not have worked without the knights because of these reasons.

   c The feudal system needed a king because...

   d The barons and bishops helped to make the feudal system work because...

2 In your opinion, was any one of these groups more important than another in the feudal system?

3 Would it have been possible to set up a feudal system in a town or a city?

4 Use a dictionary to find out the meaning of the words 'rural' and 'urban'. Which one best describes the type of society that worked within the feudal system?

You will need

Dictionary

A Basic skills: Abbreviations

Instead of writing some words in full, you can shorten or 'abbreviate' them by writing some of the letters, or just the first (initial) letters. For example, <u>Domesday Book, Volume One</u> can be shortened to <u>Domesday Bk, Vol. 1</u>. A full stop is used to show where letters are left out, words shortened, or after initials.

1   How would you abbreviate these?

   a Saint Thomas Becket   _____

   b Volume Two   _____

   c Third   _____

   d Gloucestershire   _____

   e Twentieth century   _____

   f Her Majesty   _____

   g Member of Parliament   _____

   h Versus   _____

   i Roman Catholic   _____

   j that is   _____

2   What do you think these abbreviations mean?

   a Sept.   _____

   b 1st   _____

   c 12th   _____

   d Yorks   _____

   e St John Ch 3 v 2   _____

   f AD   _____

   g BC   _____

   h William I   _____

   i <u>r.</u>1066–1087   _____

   j <u>b.</u>1027   _____

   k The Bayeux Tapestry is 70<u>m</u> long _____

   l 6 <u>am</u> Prime   _____

   m 6 <u>pm</u> Compline   _____

   n e.g.   _____

You will need

B Quick quiz

Look at page 24 in your textbook.

<u>Underline</u> the correct answer from the words or phrases in brackets.

1 The Domesday Book was a record
(of all the land in England, of what would happen if another war broke out, about the final day when God would make his judgement).

2 The Domesday Book was written by
(King William, clerks, sheriffs).

3 The information for the Domesday Book was collected by
(clerks, sheriffs, peasants).

4 All answers for the Domesday Book were sent to
(London, Winchester, Canterbury).

5 The Domesday Book is really
(one book, two books, three books).

6 The information in the Domesday Book was used to decide
(what taxes someone should pay, whether a person should go to heaven, whether a person should go to hell).

7 The Domesday Book was written in
(English, Latin, French).

8 The pages of the Domesday Book were made of
(sheepskin parchment, cowskin parchment, goatskin parchment).

9 The Domesday Book was written in
(red and black, black and blue, blue and red) ink.

10 William did not read the Domesday Book when it was completed because
(he could not read, he was dead, he preferred books on warfare).

 Questions and answers

Look at page 24 in your textbook.

The words in the Domesday Book were said on oath from representatives of each hundred (district) and each village. These are examples of the kind of questions that were asked around the country in 1085 and 1086.

	Questions	Answers
1	What is the manor called?	Yalding
2	Who owned it before 1066?	
3	Who owns it now?	
4	How many hides [the amount of land that would support one family] are there?	
5	How many ploughs in lordship?	
6	How many ploughs belong to the peasants?	
7	How many villeins are there?	
8	How many smallholders are there?	
9	How many slaves are there?	
10	How much meadow?	
11	How many mills?	
12	How many fishponds?	
13	What was the total value?	
14	What is the total value?	

Now read about the land of Richard, son of Gilbert, and see if you can answer some of the questions asked. Write them in the 'answers' column above. The first one has been done for you.

> In TWYFORD Hundred
> Richard of Tonbridge holds YALDING. Aethelred held it from King Edward. It answered for 2 hides then and now. Land for 16 ploughs. In lordship $1\frac{1}{2}$. 16 villagers with 12 smallholders have 6 ploughs. 2 churches; 15 slaves; 2 mills at 25s; 4 fisheries at 1,700 eels less 20. Meadow, 5 acres; woodland, 150 pigs. Value before 1066 and later £30; now £20, because the land has been despoiled of livestock.

D Kent, the first entry

Look at page 24 in your textbook.

Kent is the first county to be listed in the Domesday Book. The main landholders who were alive in Kent in 1086 are recorded. See if you can match the English translations to the Latin. Write the number of the Latin landowner alongside the English. The first two have been done for you.

> HIC ANNOTANT TENENTES TERRAS IN CHENT.
>
> .I. REX WILLELMVS.   .VIII. Abbatia de Gand.
>
> .II. Archieps Cantuar.   .IX. Hugo de montford.
>
> .III. 7 Monachi 7 hões ej.   .X. Comes Euftachius.
>
> .IIII. Eps Rofeceftrens.   .XI. Ricardus de Tonebrige.
>
> .V. Eps Baiocenfis.   .XII. Haimo uicecomes.
>
> .VI. Abbatia de Batailge.   .XIII. Albertus capellanus.
>
> .VII. Abbatia S Auguftini.

LIST OF LANDHOLDERS IN KENT

English				
Count Eustace	X	The Bishop of Bayeux		
Richard of Tonbridge	XI	Albert the Chaplain		
King William		Battle Abbey		
Hugh de Montfort		The Archbishop of Canterbury		
Hamo the Sheriff				
His monks and his men		Ghent Abbey		
St Augustine's Abbey		The Bishop of Rochester		

You will need

E Villages

Look at page 25 in your textbook.

Look at the picture and find as many things as you can which would have been considered taxable in medieval times.

 Words and abbreviations

Look at page 24 in your textbook.

This extract, from the Domesday Book, is about Southfleet. The translation is given alongside it.

TERRA EPI ROVECESTRE.

Eps Rofenfis ten *SVDFLETA* . p . vi . folins fe
defd . Tra . ē . xiii . car . In dnio . ē una car . 7 xxv . uilli
cū ix . bord hntes . xii . car . Ibi . vii . ferui . 7 xx . ac pti.
Silua . x . porc . Modo fe defd p . v . folins . Ibi . ē æccla.
T.R.E. 7 poft ualuit . xi . lib . Modo . xxi . lib . 7 tam redd
xxiiii . lib 7 unciā auri.

De ifto M eft in Tonebrige tantū de filua 7 de tra . qd
Ifdem eps ten *ESTANES* . T.R.E. defd p vi . folins . 7 m
p . iiii . folins . Tra . ē . xi . car . In dnio funt . ii . 7 xx . uilli
cū . xii . bord hnt . xi . car . Ibi . æccla 7 iiii . ferui . 7 Lxxii.
ac pti . 7 uñ mold de . vi . folid 7 viii . den . 7 una pifcaria
de . iii . fol 7 iiii . den . Silua . Lx . porc . T.R.E. 7 poft.
ualeb . xiii . lib . 7 m xvi . lib . 7 tam redd . xx . lib.
7 unā unciā Auri . 7 uñ Marfum . Ricard de Tonebrige
ten de ifto M tant filuæ qd ual . xv . fol.

LAND OF THE BISHOP OF ROCHESTER
The Bishop of Rochester holds SOUTHFLEET. It answered for 6 sulungs. Land for 13 ploughs. In lordship 1 plough, and 25 villagers with 9 smallholders who have 12 ploughs.
7 slaves; meadow, 20 acres; woodland, 10 pigs.
Now it answers for 5 sulungs. A church.
Value before 1066 and later £11; now £21; however, it pays £24 and an ounce of gold.
In Tonbridge there is as much woodland and land from this manor as is assessed at 20s.
The Bishop also holds STONE. Before 1066 it answered for 6 sulungs; now for 4 sulungs. Land for 11 ploughs. In lordship 2.
20 villagers with 12 smallholders have 11 ploughs.
A church; 4 slaves; meadow, 72 acres; a mill at 6s 8d; a fishery at 3s 4d; woodland, 60 pigs.
Value before 1066 and later £13; now £16; however it pays £20, an ounce of gold and a porpoise.
Richard of Tonbridge holds as much woodland from this manor as is valued at 15s.

Can you work out what these words and abbreviations mean? Write the English words alongside the Latin words.

TERRA	_____	lib	_____
EPI	_____	ten	_____
Tra	_____	bord	_____
car	_____	æccla	_____
uilli	_____	LXXII	_____
x . porc	_____	fol	_____
Ibi	_____	Lx . porc	_____
T.R.E.	_____		

 Extension activity

Look at page 24 in your textbook.

Study this artist's impression of a Domesday Book enquiry taking place in a village.

Answer the following questions in sentences.

1   Why do you think soldiers are present?

2   What are the people who record the evidence called?

3   Who do you think is seated in the chair?

4   What do you think the conversation between the two men seated next to each other is about?

5   What sort of information are the two people standing in front of the table giving the man opposite?

6   Why is the information not being put straight into a book at this time?

7   This picture is an artist's impression of events. Does it help you to understand how the information for the Domesday Book was collected?

8   Does this picture help you to understand how the Domesday Book may have been compiled? Give a reason for your answer.

You will need

A *Basic skills: Capital letters*

1   Proper nouns are the names of people and places and always use capital letters. For example, 'river' by itself does not need a capital letter as it is a common noun. 'River Humber' needs capital letters as they are proper nouns.

   a   Which one of these is correct? Put a ✓ next to the right one.

   William the conqueror   _____

   william The conqueror   _____

   William the Conqueror   _____

   William The Conqueror   _____

   William The conqueror   _____

   william the conqueror   _____

   b   Write these out correctly.

   baTTLe oF hasTings   _____

   SenLaC hiLL   _____

   king HaroLD   _____

   archBishop OF canterBury   _____

   SIR richard LuTTeraLL   _____

2   First names and surnames need capital letters:
    Richard (first name) Cooper (surname)

    Make up some medieval names by looking in your textbook and write them here.

   _____

   _____

   _____

   _____

You will need

B Quick quiz

Look at page 25 in your textbook.

1 Find and label these parts of the village:
   - water mill;
   - fields;
   - common land;
   - peasants' homes.
   - manor house;
   - church;
   - tithe barn;

2 Give one reason why the strips of land go in different directions.

3 Why is the land divided into strips and not circles?

 Surnames

Look at page 26 in your textbook.

Look at these pictures of people at work in medieval times. What surnames would you give them?

 Sorting names

Look at page 26 in your textbook.

Sort out the surnames at the bottom of this page and put them under the most suitable heading.

Military	Religious	The arts	Farming

Abbott   Stringer   Shearer   Knight

Monk   Hayward   Player   Reeve

Pike   Inkpen   Lamb   Bishop

Oxborrow   Bowman   Fiddler   Bullock

Harper   Woodward   Bowyer   Squire

Fisher   Steward

 ## Living in a cottage

Look at page 31 in your textbook.

1 Look at the outside and inside of these two cottage structures. Then read the description of the peasant's hut on page 31 in your textbook.

◄ A fourteenth-century cottage in Hagbourne, Berkshire

◄ The framework of a typical medieval cottage

2 Make a list of all the things that you think would have had a serious effect on the hygiene and health of the people who used to live in medieval cottages. If you can find 15 or more things, you deserve a high mark!

 Sickness

Look at pages 53, 54 and 69 in your textbook.

1 Explain why living near a monastery could be very useful if you became ill.

2 The monks could find out medical information from a source that the villagers had no access to. What was this source and why would the villagers not be able to make use of it?

3 Which illnesses in medieval times would you heal with the following cures:
   a Herbal remedies?
   b Blood letting?
   c Saying magic charms?
   d Prayers?
   e Special potions?

4 Some treatments seem inappropriate to us in modern times. Are there any reasons why in some cases they might have worked?

5 Why did people continue to use the treatments even when many of them did not survive?

 Extension activity

Historians use evidence to build up a picture of the past. They obtain their evidence from a variety of things. Anything they use is called a **source of evidence**. The most valuable sources are those which actually come from that period in history. Historians call these sources **primary sources**.

Here are some examples of primary sources:

- **Written documents** such as wills, rent records, tax records, court records, private letters, diaries.

- **Architecture** – buildings of that time.

- **Archaeology** – digging up evidence of that time.

- **Pictures** – books, wall-paintings, tapestries, carvings in wood and stone, statues.

Look at page 25 in your textbook. The picture is a reconstruction of a village.

1 a How many places can you see that would leave us some primary sources to study?

   b What pieces of evidence would you find in these places? In the church, for example, you might find carvings, wall-paintings, a golden goblet and stained-glass windows.

2 Make a list of buildings and primary sources you would hope to find if you went on an archaeological dig.

3 Why might it be difficult to find evidence from the village huts compared with evidence from the manor house?

A | Basic skills: Collective nouns

During the farming year each village would need a team of oxen for ploughing and a stack of hay for winter. 'Team' and 'stack' are collective nouns.

1 Complete these phrases using the words in the box.

A swarm of _____

A bale of _____

An army of _____

A tuft of _____

A sheaf of _____

A herd of _____

A gaggle of _____

A sheaf of _____

A herd of _____

A forest of _____

A congregation _____

A flock of _____

A bundle of _____

A crew of _____

| worshippers | cows | soldiers | hay | arrows | trees |
| sheep | sailors | deer | corn | grass | geese | bees | sticks |

2 Make up your own collective nouns for these groups:

A _____ of ants

A _____ of hedges

A _____ of cyclists

A _____ of babies

A _____ of caravans

A _____ of motorbikes

A _____ of teachers

A _____ of prisoners

 ## **B** | *Quick quiz*

Look at page 33 in your textbook.

1   Work out the missing crops and dates in this crop rotation grid.

West strip field	Wheat			Wheat		
			Wheat			Wheat
		Wheat			Wheat	
Crop rotation			1274			

2   Match each silhouette with the correct tool.

 Working on the farm

Look at pages 33 to 39 in your textbook.

1   What time of year is shown in the picture?

2   a What is the crop being grown in the field?
    b What could this crop be used for?

3   Write a sentence saying what:
    a the man is doing.
    b the woman is doing.

4   a Name two types of transport in the picture.
    b What might they be used for?

5   In the top half of the picture there is a building with sails.
    a What do we call these buildings?
    b What are they used for?

D | *The farming calendar*

Look at pages 33 to 39 in your textbook.

1   Look at the pictures based on a 14th-century calendar.

J

The nobleman is

_____

_____

F

The peasant is

_____

_____

M

The peasant is

_____

_____

A

The peasant is

_____

_____

M

The nobleman is

_____

_____

J

The peasant is

_____

_____

J

The peasant is

_____

_____

A

The peasant is

_____

_____

S

The peasant is

_____

_____

O

The peasant is

_____

_____

N

The peasant is

_____

_____

D

The peasant is

_____

_____

D The farming calendar (continued)

2   Fill in the months of the year on the calendar.

3   Choose the correct activity for each month and complete the calendar.

> slaughtering the pig   planting trees   cutting timber
> picking grapes   hay-mowing with a scythe
> threshing with a flail   feeding the pig on acorns
> hawking   sowing winter corn   digging a ditch
> drinking at the fireside   using a sickle to cut corn

4   a   If you had a choice, which farming task done by the peasants would you prefer to do? Explain why.

    b   Which farming task would you not like to do? Explain why.

5   The peasants in June and July are wearing different head-coverings to those shown in other months. Why do you think this is?

6   Draw the farming tools and label them.

7   *'Sow four grains in a row*
    One for the pigeon, one for the crow,
    One to rot and one to grow.'

    Look at the picture for October. Can you say why the rhyme was written in medieval times?

E Disasters

Look at pages 33 to 39 in your textbook.

The peasants' livelihood was always under threat from natural and man-made disasters.
List the natural causes under the correct seasons and add the man-made causes to build up a picture of how difficult life could be in medieval times. You may use some causes more than once.

Natural causes
drought, floods, frost,
death of livestock, plague,
death in family, illness,
poor harvest, heavy rain,
crop failure, loss of livestock

Man-made causes
warfare, crops destroyed,
house fire, mill destroyed,
heavy taxes, loss of manpower,
equipment damaged, fine for
minor misdeed, crops stolen

F Extension activity

The Church year provided a simple calendar for the villagers to work from. The main feast days or holy days corresponded with major events in the farming year. People in medieval times measured their time as that between feast days.

Festival	Peasants would...	Modern calendar
Candlemas (Feast of the Presentation of Jesus)	start spring ploughing and sowing	February 2
Lammas (St Alphonsus of Liguori)	make sure all hay was harvested	August 1
Michaelmas (Feast of Archangels)	finish harvesting and start autumn ploughing	September 29
Hallowmas (All Saints' Day)	plant winter wheat	November 1
Martinmas (St Martin of Tours)	make sure all winter wheat was planted before frosts start	November 11
Christmas Day, St Stephen's Day, St John's Day, Holy Innocents	enjoy the longest holiday as not much work to do	December 25, 26, 27 and 28

1 Why was there no long Church holiday in summer?
2 Why was the timing so important for planting seeds?
3 Each of these dates is either first or last days to do something really important. What might happen if the peasants had to keep their own calendar?
4 Why would the clergy be happy for the peasants to use the Church's calendar?
5 Peasants would not have been able to read the Church calendar if it had been written down for them. How would they have been able to follow it? What would they have to do?
6 Which modern inventions make it possible for farmers today to ignore the old Church calendar dates?

A | *Basic skills: Consonants*

Look at page 40 and 41 in your textbook.

These well-known games and pastimes have all the consonants (all the letters that are not vowels) missing. The clues will help you to fill in the missing letters.

1   O _ a _ _ e _ a _ _ _ e _ o _ _ (fruits)

2   _ i _ e a _ _ _ e e _ (count to ten)

3   _ i _ _ a _ i _ _ o' _ o _ e _ (sneeze)

4   _ _ i _ _ _ a _ ' _ _ u _ _ (why not woman?)

5   _ o _ _ _ o _ _ _ (you need numbers and a pebble)

6   _ o o _ _ a _ _ (you must know this English game)

7   _ i _ _ _ - _ a _ _ (think of pork)

8   _ _ e _ _ _ i _ _ (not recommended for bony people)

9   _ e a _ - _ a i _ i _ _ (considered cruel now)

10   _ _ i _ _ e _ (grasshopper)

11   _ _ e _ _ (checkmate)

12   _ _ a u _ _ _ _ (close the door to keep these out)

13   _ a _ _ _ a _ _ o _ (think of pork again)

14   _ a _ _ _ _ a _ i _ i e _ (better than sad ones)

15   _ u _ _ _ (a town in England)

Answers:
1 Oranges and lemons
2 Hide and seek
3 Ring a ring o' roses
4 Blind man's buff
5 Hop scotch
6 Football
7 Piggy-back
8 Wrestling
9 Bear-baiting
10 Cricket
11 Chess
12 Draughts
13 Backgammon
14 Happy families
15 Rugby

B Quick quiz

Look at pages 40 and 41 in your textbook.

1 Which pastime requires a pole? _____

2 How many people are needed to play:

   a pick-a-back? _____

   b wrestling? _____

3 Make a list of the games mentioned on pages 40 and 41 which require a ball.

   _____

   _____

   _____

   _____

4 **a** How many stringed instruments can you see on page 40? _____

   b Name two of the stringed instruments. _____

   _____

5 How many sports can you see girls taking part in? _____

6 Make a list of the games mentioned on these pages which are still played today.

   _____

   _____

   _____

   _____

You will need
Dictionary

C Football and cock-fighting

Look at page 41 in your textbook.

Read this extract about football and cock-fighting and then answer the questions.

> Six men citizens and tapisers, and two others, citizens and parishioners of St Denis Bakchurche, were forced to give a bond of twenty pounds to the city chamberlain for their good behaviour towards 'the kind and good men of the mystery of Cordwainers' and that they would not collect money for a football nor money called 'cocksilver' for cockerels, hens, capons, or other birds, or thrash* any cockerel in the streets or lanes of the city. (March 4, 1409)

Whipping or thrashing the cockerel was a sport practised at wakes and fairs, in which carters, armed with whips, were blindfolded and set round a cockerel to whip at it.

1   Find out the meaning of the following words:
   a citizen;
   b parishioner;
   c carter;
   d chamberlain;
   e wake;
   f bond.

2   What do you think had happened to force the tapisers and parishioners to give a bond for good behaviour?

3   Explain what might happen if a game of football got out of hand in the streets of a medieval town.

4   List some precautions that are taken today to prevent football games and crowds from getting out of hand.

5   Cock-fighting still happens today. Explain why 'thrashing the cockerel' might be considered to be an even crueller sport.

D Extension activity

To proclaim a friendly joust, 15th century
We heralds of arms, bearing coats of arms, here proclaim to all gentlemen
of family and of arms that there are six gentlemen of family and of arms who
because of their great desire and honor have agreed to appear on the third
day of next May before the high, mighty, and worshipful ladies and
gentlewomen of this high and most honorable court, and to joust against all
corners from nine of the bell before noon until six of the bell in the
afternoon.

Then a diamond worth forty pounds is to be given to the stranger knight
who in the opinion of the said ladies and gentlewomen is the best jouster,
and to the next best a ruby worth twenty pounds, and to the third best
jouster a sapphire worth ten pounds.

And on that day there shall be officers of arms to take the measure of
their spears as they are fitted out, that is, with coronal, vamplate and
grapers* all of the size that they shall joust with. The said comers may take
the length of the said spears in consultation with the said officers of arms,
who shall be impartial toward all parties on the said day.

Coronal, vamplate and grapers are names given to various parts of equipment

1 Why do you think the women were allowed to choose
   the best knight?
2 Who were the heralds and what was their job?
3 What was a 'coat of arms'?
4 How long did the jousting match last?
5 Was there any limit to the number of challenges the six
   knights could face during the day?
6 Why was it necessary to have an official to measure the length
   of the spears (lances)?
7 What would the six knights gain by taking part in the joust?
8 What would the three best stranger knights gain by partaking
   in the joust?
9 Some knights became very rich and famous by jousting.
   Crowds went specially to see their favourites.
   a Which modern sporting hero would you take the trouble to
     go and see?
   b Why are they so special?
   c Which sport do they do?

You will need

A Basic skills: Doubles

Words are often used together to give greater emphasis. See if you can complete these phrases, choosing from the words in the box. The first one has been done for you.

cry   ~~punishment~~   ends   nail   thin
shoulders   tumble   kin   low
furious   go   again   key   order
square   only   tongs   void   rave
soul   tear   means   call

crime and **punishment**

hue and _____

beck and _____

high and _____

kith and _____

rough and _____

law and _____

lock and _____

fair and _____

wear and _____

thick and _____

head and _____

rant and _____

fast and _____

odds and _____

ways and _____

touch and _____

time and _____

one and _____

tooth and _____

hammer and _____

heart and _____

null and _____

You will need

B *Quick quiz*

Look at pages 42 and 43 in your textbook.

Match each key word to the right definition with a line.

Key word

Accuse

Accuser

Trial

Jury

Court

Verdict

Guilty

Not guilty

Punishment

Defend

Prosecute

Definition

| The decision made at the end of the trial |

| Something you have to suffer if you have done wrong |

| Responsible for doing something wrong |

| The time spent in court, while others decide if he has or has not done something wrong |

| To say that someone has done something wrong |

| A group of people who decide if you are guilty or not guilty |

| To protect someone in court |

| To make someone go to court so that they can be punished if they have done wrong |

| The place where people decide whether someone is guilty of breaking the law |

| A person who blames someone of doing something wrong |

| Innocent of committing a crime |

C Punishment

Look at page 42 in your textbook.

In this modern-day drawing, the man on the sledge has sold bad fish.

1 How is the man being punished?

2 What are the onlookers doing to him?

3 Why do you think the fishmonger has sold bad fish?

4 What do you think would have happened to this man if someone had died from eating his bad fish?

5 What punishment might he receive today if:

   a he sold bad fish?

   b someone died from eating his bad fish?

6 How did people preserve food in medieval times?

7 How do we keep food fresh today?

D A *public execution*

Look at page 43 in your textbook.

1 How is this man being executed?

2 Do you think this man is poor or wealthy? Give reasons for your answer.

3 Why is he being executed in public?

4 Why do you think there is a large crowd watching?

5 What crime do you think he might have committed?

6 Name one other person on the scaffold and say why he is there.

 Trials

Look at page 44 in your textbook.

The Normans introduced trial by ordeal and trial by combat.
Complete the boxes below using your own words to
1   describe the 'trial';
2   say what would happen if you were found to be guilty;
3   say whether you think this form of trial is fair or not;
4   say how you would improve on these trials to make them fairer.

	Trial by ordeal	Trial by combat
	For peasants	For barons and nobles
1	Ordeal by fire: the accused would...	The accused and the accuser would...
2	If found guilty...	If found guilty...
3	This trial was fair/unfair because...	This trial was fair/unfair because...
4	I would make this trial fairer by...	I would make this trial fairer by...

F Extension activity

Read these two extracts and answer the questions.

> KEEPING THE CITY
>
> **Hue and cry by horn and voice, 1302**
>
> (Six men [servants and young men] were accused of attacking and assaulting the watch of Walbrook Ward, June 14, 1302.)
>
> Afterwards on Thursday a jury... found on oath that the defendants committed the assault when midnight was striking at St Paul's, and were captured after the hue and cry had been raised by horn and voice and the neighboring wards had come to help... [The young men] had filled an empty cask with stones on Monday midnight and set it rolling through Gracechurch Street to London Bridge to the great terror of the neighbours. The young men were arrested and put in the Tun [prison].

1 a Was 'the watch' a small clock, a place or a person?

   b How did the jury know it was midnight when the crime was committed?

   c What is a hue and cry and how can you raise it by horn and voice?

   d Do you think the men were captured easily?

   e What do you think was in the cask when it was full?

> **Curfew bells, 1370**
>
> Proclamation was made December 4, 44 Edward III [1370]... that no one wander in the City after curfew sounded at the churches of St Mary-le-Bow, Barking Church in Tower Ward, St Bride, and St Giles without Cripplegate, unless he be of good repute and carry a light, on pain of imprisonment.
>
> That no taverner or brewer keep open house after curfew sounded at the above churches, and that curfew be not sounded at any other church later than at the above churches.

2 a What is a curfew?

   b Why do you think a curfew was necessary in the City of London?

   c What sort of person is a person of 'good repute'?

   d Why does London Corporation want people to carry a light?

   e What jobs do a taverner and brewer do?

   f Why are they specifically mentioned in this extract?

   g Why were other churches not allowed to ring the bells for curfew at a later time?

3 By studying both extracts, do you think law and order was or was not taken seriously in the 14th century?

A Basic skills: Key words

A key word is one which is essential to the meaning of a sentence. For example, in the sentence

✓   ✗ ✓ ✗ ✗   ✓   ✓

Ordeal by **fire** was a **common punishment**

the key words are 'ordeal', 'fire', 'common' and 'punishment'.

Finding the key words will help you to make notes. Find the key words in the following sentences.

Sentence	Key words
The church and the priest were the centre of the village.	_____
To help with the upkeep of the church, the villagers gave a tenth of what they produced – usually crops or animals – to the priest as a tax, or tithe.	_____
The wealthy could save their souls and go to heaven by donating money to the Church to build monasteries, nunneries and cathedrals.	_____
Over the centuries the Church grew richer and became the largest landowner in Europe.	_____
But its real strength lay in the power it had over people's minds.	_____

B Quick quiz

Look at pages 46 to 50 in your textbook.

1 If you lived a godly life, where would you go when you died?

2 For what reasons might someone think they would go to hell?

3 What was purgatory?

4 What was the main language used by the Church?

5 Which person was the Supreme Head of the Church on earth?

6 Who were the most powerful churchmen in each country?

7 Why was ribbed vaulting given that description?

8 Why were Bible scenes painted on church walls?

9 Name two ways that churches were lit.

10 Name three types of buildings used by people who joined the Church.

11 What was the tithe?

12 Could anyone become a priest or a nun?

C Church architecture

Look at page 49 in your textbook.

To which century and style of church and cathedral architecture do these belong?

_____ century

_____ style

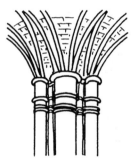

_____ century

_____ style

_____ century

_____ style

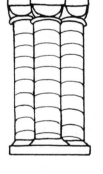

_____ century

_____ style

_____ century

_____ style

_____ century

_____ style

_____ century

_____ style

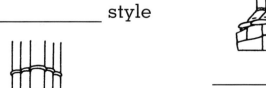

_____ century

_____ style

_____ century

_____ style

_____ century

_____ style

_____ century

_____ style

D Monastery services

Look at pages 50 to 56 in your textbook.

1   Make a list of all the services a medieval monastery and monks offered. These diagrams will help you.

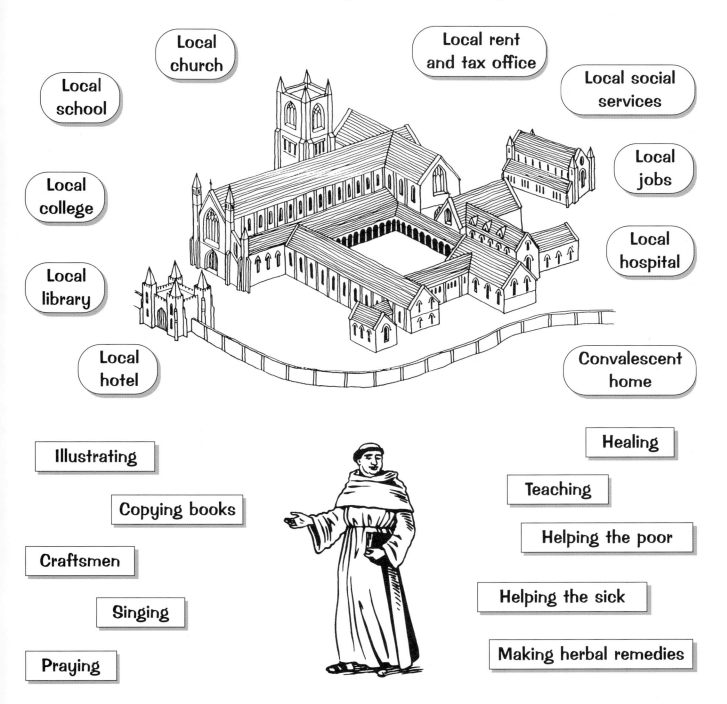

Local church

Local rent and tax office

Local school

Local social services

Local college

Local jobs

Local library

Local hospital

Local hotel

Convalescent home

Illustrating

Healing

Copying books

Teaching

Craftsmen

Helping the poor

Singing

Helping the sick

Praying

Making herbal remedies

2   Now make another list of how many separate organisations and buildings are needed in a modern town to do the same work!

You will need

E Monks' winter timeline

Look at the pages 51 and 52 in your textbook.

1 Cut out the boxes below and arrange them in time order.

2 Write a sentence underneath each box to describe what the monks would do at that time.

2.30am	9am	4pm	3am	7am
2pm	6pm	6am	12 noon	6.30pm
10am	8am	3pm	11am	5pm

 You could become a monk!

Look at pages 50 to 55 in your textbook.

1 Read the job vacancy poster below.

JOB VACANCY

The Church needs a dedicated monk. The successful applicant will:
- have part of his head shaved regularly.
- be guaranteed a job for life.
- live in one place all his life.
- own nothing.
- go to church seven times a day.
- eat twice a day.
- not be allowed to speak whilst eating.
- wear rough clothes.
- go to bed as soon as it gets dark.
- sleep on a straw mattress in a dormitory.
- spend one year as a novice (learner).
- always do as he is told.

2 Now read the information on the next sheet about some of the different religious orders that monks could join.

3 Design a job vacancy poster for one of the orders. Include the information given on both pages of this worksheet.

4 Draw a picture of a monk on your poster.

 F *You could become a monk! (continued)*

Cistercian order

Their monasteries were built far away from towns. The monks worked very hard. As well as farming, they had to cut down forests, drain marshes and sometimes even dig coal out of hillsides. The monks wore a grey-white cloak made from undyed sheep's wool. This is why they were called 'white monks'.

Carthusian order

The monks spent most of their lives alone. They lived in separate rooms and cooked their own food. They only met together for a meal on Sunday and at church services. Even when they met they never spoke to each other and kept their hoods over their faces. There were no nuns in this order. The monks could worship God in peace and calm. They could get away from everyday life.

Benedictine order

The monks had to do as they were told. They lived in absolute poverty. They were not allowed sexual relationships. Women could join the order if they lived in convents and never married. They were called 'black monks' because they wore a black cloak and hood.

 Festivals and processions

Festivals and processions were an important part of the Church year. Work out from the descriptions which days fit the spaces.

Cut out the days from the third sheet and stick them in.

Spring sowing started on this date. Churches and houses were decorated with extra candles.

Villeins began to get ready for Easter. They would go to church and confess their sins to the priest. They would then be 'shriven' (forgiven). Today we call this day 'Pancake Day'.

This day began the Church season known as Lent, which lasted 40 days. Christians remembered the 40 days that Jesus spent in the wilderness being tempted by the devil. People stopped eating meat as Jesus stopped eating meat. There would be a special service when the priest made a mark with ash on each person's forehead. This was to remind them that one day they would die and turn to dust and ashes.

This day comes from the Latin word 'mandatum', which means a command or order. It is the day before Good Friday. In medieval times kings and bishops washed the feet of some old people and gave them clothing, food and money. This was because Jesus washed his disciples' feet at the Last Supper.

You will need

G Festivals and processions (continued)

This day was to remember the day that Jesus was crucified. The priest in the village church would hold a solemn service when all the statues and pictures would be covered with black cloth as a sign of mourning.

This day celebrated Jesus rising from the dead and was the most important holy day of the Church year. The church was decorated with flowers and the village well would be decorated with fresh green branches. As a symbol of this re-birth, children were given real eggs painted in red and black.

This marked the time when Jesus's disciples were filled with the Holy Spirit and came seven weeks after Easter. People enjoyed feasts and performed religious plays. At this time, as well as at Christmas and Easter, all the king's nobles went to court to demonstrate their loyalty.

On this day the Church told people to remember the dead who had lived good and saintly lives. Church bells rang in memory of the dead and villagers made 'soul cakes' to eat.

You will need

G Festivals and processions (continued)

Sunday

Wednesday

Saint's

Friday

Whit

Day

Thursday

Good

Easter

Ash

Shrove

Sunday

Maundy

All

Tuesday

Candlemas

 Joining the Church

Look at pages 50 to 55 in your textbook.

1 Read these two lists carefully.

Personality	Practicality
Honesty	Promotion by ability
Sense of humour	Guaranteed food for life
Intelligence	Guaranteed place to live
Hardworking	Guaranteed income
Humility	for life
Caring	Learn to read and write
Trustworthy	Not subject to king's law
Loving	Do not fight in wars
Patient	Belong to biggest
Saving your soul	organisation in Europe
Belief in God	Do something you
Kind	believe in
Sense of duty	Do work for the king
Obedient	

2 Which things from the two lists would Church leaders expect from those people who wished to join the Church?

3 Do you think people who wished to join the Church had one main reason or a mixture of reasons?

4 In an organisation as big as the Church, why would it include 'good' and 'bad' monks, nuns and priests?

1 Monastery jobs

Look at pages 50 to 55 in your textbook.

1 Complete the chart below.

Job	Job description	Type of personality needed
Abbot		
Cellarer		
Kitchener		
Chamberlain		
Precentor		
Infirmarian		
Almoner		
Hosteller		
Sacrist		

2 From this list, which job would most suit your own personality?

J Chaucer and the Church

Geoffrey Chaucer, a famous poet of the 14th century, wrote about two members of the Church. Read about them and then answer the questions.

Chaucer's parson

There was a good man of religion who was a poor parson of a town but he was rich in holy thoughts and works. He was also an educated man, a scholar who knew and taught the Gospel and Bible thoroughly. He often gave away his money rather than take his tithe. He never neglected in rain, thunder, sickness or trouble to visit the rich and poor of his parish on foot. He taught the Word of Christ and his twelve apostles – but first he followed it himself.

Chaucer's pardoner

In his bag he had a pillowcase which he said was Our Lady's veil. He said he had a piece of sail from St Peter's boat. He had in a glass some pig's bones. With these 'relics' whenever he found a poor country parson he got himself more money in one day than the parson got in two months. And so with false flattery and tricks he made monkeys of the parson and the people.

1 Geoffrey Chaucer lived at this time. Do you think he was writing about real people he knew or about people he had heard about?

2 Chaucer's writing reflects his own opinions of his two characters. Write out which words or phrases are his <u>opinion</u>.

3 What is the difference between an opinion and a fact?

K Extension activity

Read the following extract about the importance of the Church in the lives of ordinary people, and then answer the questions.

> The oaths of the people are religious, their methods of calculating time are religious, their principal landlords – bishop and prior – are religious, their inns are religious houses, their feasts and their plays, their fairs and processions all are connected with religion; they begin their wills, 'In the name of our Lord Jesus Christ, amen.' They believed that the be all and the end all of life was not to be found in this world. Dimly and childishly and clumsily, through their clasped fingers, on their bent knees, in their language and legends past their hard tasks and taskmasters they were looking ahead to the indescribable loveliness of the paradise of God.
>
> (From *History of County Durham* by Sir Timothy Eden)

1 Explain why people at that time used the expression 'Mother Church' to describe their view of the Church.

2 How, according to the author, did the people manage to put up with so much hardship in their lives?

3 The Church offered both practical and spiritual help to the people. Which, in your opinion, was the most important? Explain why.

 A *Basic skills: Commas*

When there is a list of words in a sentence, each word is separated from the next by a comma. For example:

We will need pencils, rulers, rubbers and glue.

The last word in the list is usually joined to the list by 'and' instead of a comma.

Make these into proper sentences by putting commas in the right places.

1   Famous shrines included St Alban's Cathedral Durham Cathedral Walsingham Bury St Edmunds and Westminster Abbey.

2   Some important dates in Becket's life were 1155 1162 1164 and 1170.

3   The four knights who murdered Becket were Reginald FitzUrse William de Tracy Hugh de Morville and Richard the Breton.

4   Pilgrims left candles walking sticks iron chairs children's clothes swords spears lances and wax images at the shrine of St Thomas Cantilupe.

5   People went on pilgrimages to be healed to pray to kiss the tomb to give thanks to God to see the sights and to go on holiday.

B Quick quiz

1 Label the picture below with the following words:

Becket   **monk**   **knight**
altar   **altar cloth**

2 Why is this archbishop being killed?

_____

_____

_____

_____

_____

3 a Who is being punished?

_____

b Why is he being punished?

_____

_____

_____

4 a Who is in this coffin?

_____

b Why do the monks look sad?

_____

_____

 True or false

Look at pages 57, 58 and 59 in your textbook.

Consider whether these statements are true or false, or if there is not enough evidence from the text to decide. Fill in the table with your answers.

		True	False	Not enough evidence
1	Becket loved hunting.			
2	The Archbishop of Canterbury was the most powerful man in the country.			
3	You could be sentenced to death in the Church court.			
4	Henry II wanted all criminals to be punished.			
5	Becket and the King never argued.			
6	Becket said only God could punish members of the Church.			
7	Becket believed the King was more powerful than God.			
8	It was a good thing to be excommunicated from the Church.			
9	Becket plotted to kill the King.			
10	The King sent six knights to kill Becket.			
11	Becket and his friends had a swordfight with the knights.			
12	Two of the knights were killed in the fight.			
13	Halley's Comet was seen by people in Britain at the same time that Becket was killed.			
14	Henry II blamed everyone but himself for Becket's death.			

 Becket's life

Cut out these pictures and put them in the right order to tell the story of Thomas Becket. Use your textbook to find out the dates and write a few sentences about each picture.

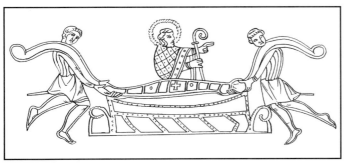

E The murder of Becket

What observations can you make about the similarities and differences in these pictures? Write down your observations. For example:

1   The pictures all show four knights.

2   Pictures 1, 2 and 4 show Thomas Becket's hat falling off.

3   I can see the altar cloth in pictures 2, 3 and 4.

F | Dilemmas

Henry II and Thomas Becket were faced with difficult decisions.
What might they have thought at the time? Fill in the bubbles
using the ideas in the box below to help you.

Reasons to get rid of Thomas

_____

_____

_____

_____

_____

_____

Reasons to keep Thomas

_____

_____

_____

_____

_____

_____

Reasons not to be loyal to Henry

_____

_____

_____

_____

_____

_____

Reasons to be loyal to Henry

_____

_____

_____

_____

_____

_____

Some ideas to help you

respect	obey God	stubbornness	be a good leader
loyalty	old friend	follow your conscience	trust
selfishness	things change	new priorities	
responsibilities	make an example	pride	

G Can you stop Becket's murder?

You have heard of the plot by the four knights to kill Becket. You and your partner decide to send an urgent message to warn him of the knight's plans. The message must be sent in code.

1   Decide what you will say to Becket – keep it short.

2   a   Think of a way of coding your message. This is an example.

Message:

Get out of Canterbury tonight.

They are coming to murder you!

A simple code could be:

a	b	c	d	e	f	g	h	i	j	k	l	m	n	o	p	q	r	s	t	u	v	w	x	y	z
z	y	x	w	v	u	t	s	r	q	p	o	n	m	l	k	j	i	h	g	f	e	d	c	b	a

The message in code would be:

Tvg lfg lu xzmgviyfb glmrtsg.

Gsrb ziv xlnrmt gl nfiwvi blf!

b   Invent your own code and get another pair to translate your message. Don't forget that they will need to know how your code works!

You will need

H Picturing the murder

Look at page 59 in your textbook.

Describe what is happening in the picture below.

1 Does Becket look scared?

_____

_____

2 What is he doing?

_____

_____

3 What are the knights doing?

_____

_____

4 Do the knights look happy killing Becket?

_____

_____

1 An eyewitness account

Look at page 59 in your textbook.

Eyewitness statement: Thomas Becket's murder

Canterbury Constabulary

Your name _____

Describe in detail what you saw:

_____

_____

_____

_____

_____

_____

_____

_____

_____

_____

_____

_____

_____

_____

1, _____ **(name) truly believe this to be an accurate record of the events.**

Signed _____

Things to include in your statement:

● **Facts**: When? Where? Who? Why?

● **People**: Clothes, features, voices, movement

● **Atmosphere**: Time of day, weather, what you were doing?

J Why was Becket killed?

Look at pages 58 to 60 in your textbook.

Why did King Henry II want Becket killed? Nine possible reasons are given on the second page of this worksheet.

The most important reason will be at the top of the diamond shape and the least important reason at the bottom.

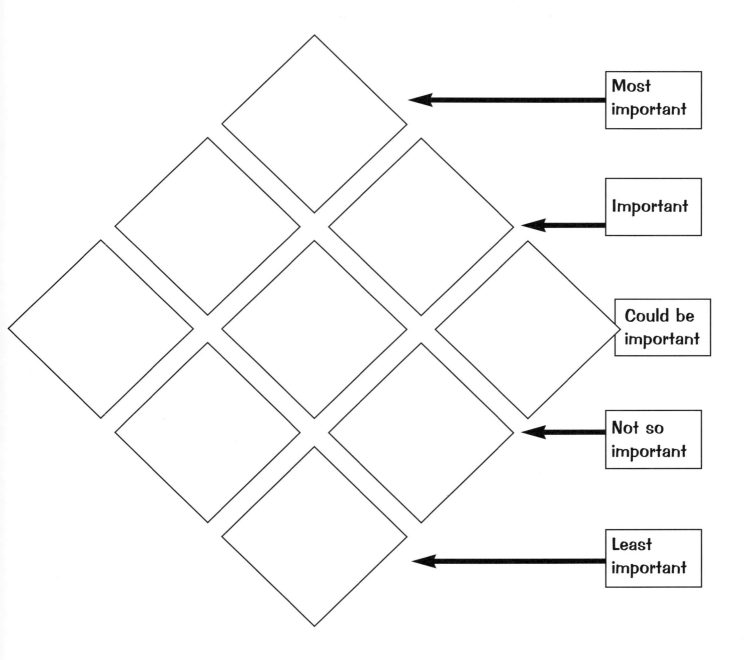

Most important

Important

Could be important

Not so important

Least important

You will need

J Why was Becket killed? (continued)

Cut out and stick these reasons in the order of importance on the diamond shape on the first page of this worksheet.

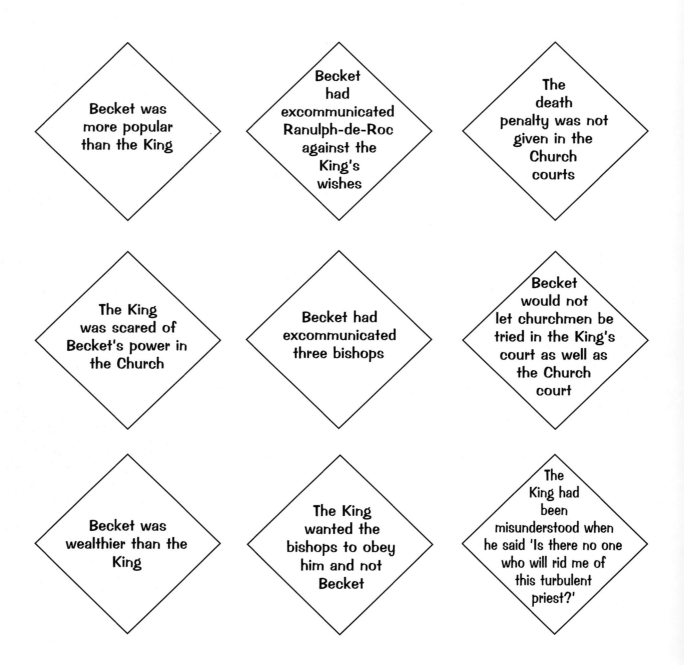

Becket was more popular than the King

Becket had excommunicated Ranulph-de-Roc against the King's wishes

The death penalty was not given in the Church courts

The King was scared of Becket's power in the Church

Becket had excommunicated three bishops

Becket would not let churchmen be tried in the King's court as well as the Church court

Becket was wealthier than the King

The King wanted the bishops to obey him and not Becket

The King had been misunderstood when he said 'Is there no one who will rid me of this turbulent priest?'

K *Pilgrims and pilgrimages*

Look at page 61 in your textbook.

Pilgrimages were popular for many reasons. Can you think why?

Pilgrims would like to go on pilgrimages because

_____

_____

_____

The monks at the shrines would welcome pilgrims because

_____

_____

_____

_____

Stallholders, businessmen and innkeepers would like pilgrims because

_____

_____

_____

The leaders of the Catholic Church would approve of pilgrimages because

_____

_____

_____

_____

 The Canterbury Tales

Geoffrey Chaucer, a famous poet who lived in the 14th century, wrote a book called *The Canterbury Tales*. He wrote in English although the spellings are different from the ones you know today.

Read each passage out loud, then see if you can translate them into modern English.

1 Here Chaucer describes a group of pilgrims who set off from London to visit the shrine of Thomas Becket in Canterbury.

> And specially from every shire's ende
> of Engelond to Caunterbury they wende,
> The hooly blisful martir for to seke,
> That hem hath holpen whan that they were seeke.

My translation

_____

_____

_____

_____

2 This is the description of a young squire, the son of a knight.

> With hym ther was his sone, a young Squier
> He was as fressh as is the month of May.
> Short was his gowne, with sleves long and wyde.
> Wel koude he sitte on hors and faire ryde.

My translation

_____

_____

_____

_____

[L] The Canterbury Tales (continued)

3 This is from the tale of the Wife of Bath.

> *A good wif was ther of bisidé Bathe*
> *She was a worthy womman al hir lyve:*
> *And thries hadde she been at Jerusalem;*
> *She hadde passed many a straunge strem;*
> *At Rome she hadde been, and at Boloigne.*

My translation

_____

_____

_____

_____

_____

4 Here is a description of the Prioress.

> *Ther was also a nonne, a prioresse*
> *At mete wel y-taught was she with alle:*
> *She leet no morsel from hir lippes falle,*
> *Ne wette hir fyngres in hir sauce depe;*
> *Wel koude she carie a morsel and wel kepe*
> *That no drope ne fille upon hire brest.*

My translation

_____

_____

_____

_____

_____

You will need

M *Visiting a shrine*

Look at pages 60 to 63 in your textbook.

Select a shrine to visit. Write a short account of your pilgrimage. You may wish to include some or all of the following details in your account.

- Why are you going on a pilgrimage?
- Why have you chosen this particular shrine?
- What relics are at the shrine?
- How did you travel to the shrine (on foot, by horse...)?
- Who were you travelling companions? Were they all men?
- What dangers did you face on the journey?
- Where did you sleep overnight?
- What offering did you leave at the shrine?
- What 'badge' did you bring back as a souvenir of the pilgrimage?
- What shrine do you plan to visit next and why do you want to go there?

A record of my pilgrimage to the shrine of

_____

_____

_____

_____

_____

_____

_____

_____

_____

 Extension activity

1   Look at pages 57 and 58 in your textbook.

a   Was King Henry II right to want to change the law so that members of the Church could be tried in the King's court? Give a reason for your answer.

b   Why did Becket say no to the King's request to have members of the Church tried in the King's court?

c   Why did Becket decide to wear a goats' hair shirt and give up his rich way of life after becoming Archbishop of Canterbury?

d   What does 'excommunicate' mean and why was it seen as a terrible punishment?

e   Why did Becket excommunicate three bishops?

f   Give two reasons why Becket and the King quarrelled after Becket had been made Archbishop of Canterbury.

g   What is the King alleged to have said which was to lead to the murder of Becket?

h   What do you think the King meant when he said 'who will rid me of this turbulent priest'?

2   Look at page 59 in your textbook.

a   Why did the four knights threaten Becket? What do you think they said to him?

b   Why did the monks persuade Becket to go into the cathedral?

c   Why did the knights want Becket outside of the cathedral?

d   What did the four knights hope to gain by killing Becket?

e   What 'natural event' is said to have happened when Becket was killed? What was its meaning to the people of England?

3   Look at page 60 in your textbook.

a   Becket's burial place became a shrine. What is a shrine and what sort of miracles were said to have happened at Becket's shrine?

b   Why did Henry II take the blame for Becket's death? Do you think the King loved Becket as a friend, or was he scared of God's punishment or public outrage?

 A *Basic skills: Capital letters, commas and full stops*

The passage below needs capital letters (ABC, and so on), commas (,) and full stops (.) to be inserted for it to make sense. Copy the passage, inserting capital letters, commas and full stops as you go.

in 1070 a tribe of muslim turks captured jerusalem pilgrims returning from the holy city told stories of beatings torture and persons being sold into slavery the pope was angry and pleaded with nobles and barons to free jerusalem from the infidels.

the first part of the crusade was not successful and many of the crusaders were killed the second part was more successful it had a well organised army this army had a great deal of food armour weapons and tents these crusaders faced many dangers including dysentery typhoid scurvy starvation and possible death in battle after many adventures they forced their way into the city of jerusalem murdering many of the muslims jews women and children they went to the church of the holy sepulchre to give thanks for their victory

You will need

B Quick quiz

Look at pages 63, 64 and 67 in your textbook.

1   Who founded the religion of Islam? _____

2   Pope Urban II wanted _____ or peace.

3   Constantinople was capital of the _____ Empire.

4   What badge did the Crusader knights wear?

_____

5   Give two reasons why a knight would fight in the Crusaders.

a _____

b _____

6   What does the word 'crusade' mean?

_____

7   Name two of the countries that Crusader armies came from to fight the Turks.

a _____ b _____

8   Name one disease that some of the knights died from.

_____

9   Which city did the Crusaders capture in 1098?

_____

10 Which city did the Crusaders capture in 1099?

_____

11 Which church in Jerusalem marks Christ's tomb?

_____

12 Name the two 'fighting monk' brotherhoods.

a _____

b _____

You will need

C *Labels*

Look at pages 64 to 67 in your textbook.

The labels for these two pictures have become mixed up. Label each picture correctly.

chain-mail	spurs	scimitar	lance
CRUSADER	dagger	**SARACEN**	standard
sword	no body armour	round shield	
	short bow	surcoat	

D The First Crusade part two

Look at pages 65 and 66 in your textbook.

This is a picture diary of the second part of the First Crusade.
Fill in what happened at these places.

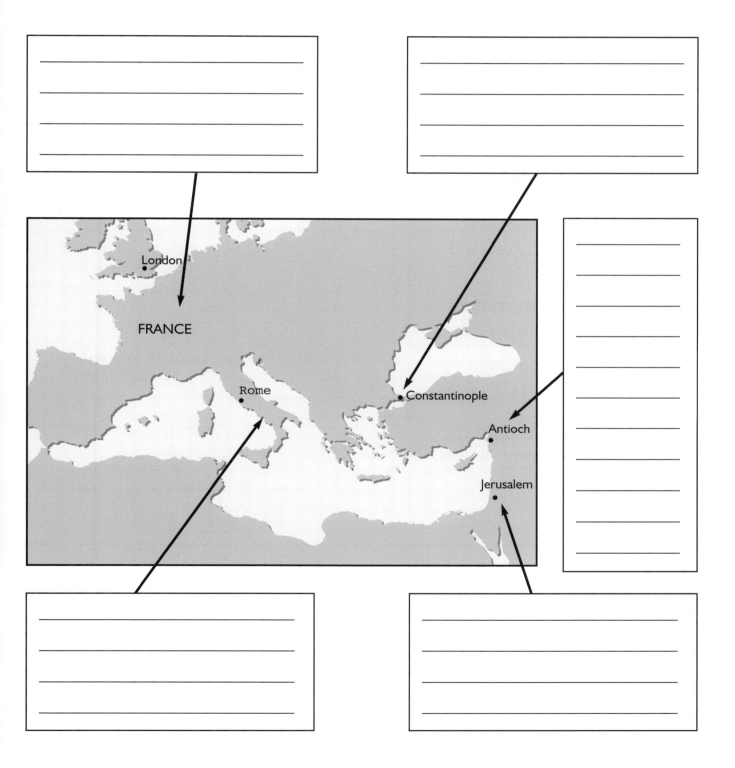

E Effects of the Crusades

Look at pages 68 to 71 in your textbook.

Quite often in history the effects of a war do not always become apparent until the fighting is over.

Look at these three consequences of the Crusades. Use the page numbers to help you find out how Europe was effected by the Crusades and what the results were for the people. The first one has been done for you.

Medicine (pages 68 and 71)

The **effects** in Europe were...

better understanding and knowledge of illness and disease.

The **results** for Europeans were... more hospitals and improved treatment for patients. Scientists and doctors looked for new and better ways to treat illness.

Navigation (page 70)

The **effects** in Europe were...

_____

_____

_____

_____

_____

The **results** for Europeans were...

_____

_____

_____

_____

Trade (page 70)

The **effects** in Europe were... _____

_____

The **results** for Europeans were... _____

_____

_____

F | Extension activity

The following extract has been adapted from Sir Walter Scott's novel, *The Talisman*, which was written in 1832.

> It was Richard's two-handed sword that attracted the attention of Saladin. 'Had I not seen it used in battle, I would not believe that any human could use it. Might I see you strike a blow with it?'
>
> Richard looked around and saw a steel mace with a steel handle an inch and a half thick. He lifted up the sword and swung it over his head, bringing it down onto the steel handle and cutting it cleanly in two.
>
> Saladin, knowing that he could not match the strength of Richard, looked for something else to impress him. He saw a silk cushion lying on the floor. 'Can your weapon cut that cushion?' he asked.
>
> 'No sword on earth can cut that which gives no resistance,' the King replied.
>
> 'Watch, then,' said Saladin, and he drew his scimitar sword, which was curved, narrow and razor-sharp. It was clearly a superb weapon and, with it, he gently cut the cushion in two.

1 How did Richard demonstrate brute force?

2 Was Saladin impressed by Richard's use of the two-handed sword?

3 What did Richard mean when he said, 'No sword on earth can cut that which gives no resistance'?

4 What was so special about Saladin's scimitar that it could cut through the cushion?

5 What lesson did Saladin teach Richard?

6 How does this extract show a difference between the European and Middle Eastern ways of solving a problem?

A Basic skills: Compound words

Inventors often took one thing or invention and made another. For example, wheel and water = water-wheel. See if you can match these. The first one has been done for you.

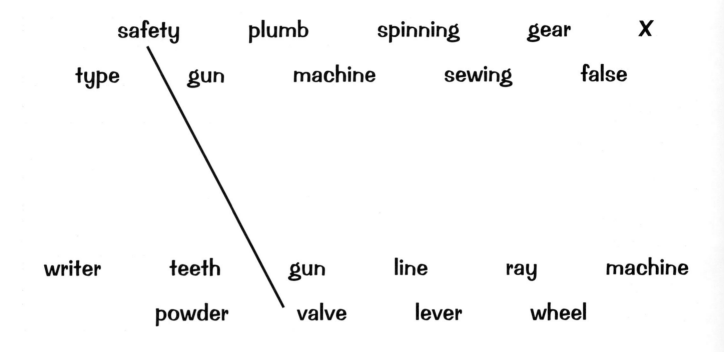

safety   plumb   spinning   gear   **X**

type   gun   machine   sewing   false

writer   teeth   gun   line   ray   machine

powder   valve   lever   wheel

---

fire   wind   printing   wall   cross   alarm

horse   wheel   stained   magnetic

clock   bow   barrow   glass   painting

compass   mill   work   press   shoe

You will need

B Quick quiz

Look at pages 70 and 71 in your textbook.

1 Write in the 'function' column what each of these inventions was used for.

Invention	Function
Gunpowder	
Spectacles	
Printing press	
Astrolabe	
Magnetic sea compass	
Plumbrod	
Lateen sail	

2 Below is a list of common inventions that we use today. Can you say what each invention is used for?

Invention	Function
X-ray machine	
Battery	
Refrigerator	
Television	
Electric shower	
Computer	
Car	
Telephone	

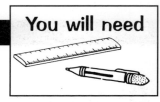

C When were they invented?

Below is a list of common items. <u>Underline</u> the date when you think they were invented. *c.* is short for 'circa' and means 'about'.

1 Wheelbarrow (*c.*200–300   *c.*500–600   *c.*800–900)

2 Horseshoe (*c.*50   *c.*150   *c.*250)

3 Saddle (*c.*25–220   *c.*225–420   *c.*525–720)

4 Chess (100   600   900)

5 Paper money (*c.*200   *c.*500   *c.*700)

6 Magnetic compass (790   990   1090)

7 Spectacles (1286   1486   1686)

8 Longbow (650   950   1250)

9 Alarm clock (1350   1750   1950)

10 Wallpaper (1509   1709   1909)

11 Telescope (*c.*990   *c.*1290   *c.*1590)

12 Pencil (1065   1565   1965)

13 Umbrella (637   1037   1637)

14 Submarine (1424   1624   1824)

15 False teeth (1770   1870   1970)

16 Sandwich (1762   1862   1962)

17 Canned food (1611   1711   1811)

18 Bicycle (1739   1839   1939)

19 Postage stamp (1740   1840   1940)

20 Tin opener (1655   1765   1855)

Answers:
1 *c.*200–300; **2** *c.*50; **3** *c.*25–220; **4** 600; **5** *c.*700; **6** 1090; **7** 1286;
8 1250; **9** 1350; **10** 1509; **11** *c.*1590; **12** 1565; **13** 1637; **14** 1624;
15 1770; **16** 1762; **17** 1811; **18** 1839; **19** 1840; **20** 1855.

D Which treatment?

Look at page 69 in your textbook.

You have gangrene in your right leg and it requires urgent treatment. Who can help you? In the box is a list of some treatments for your gangrene.

Choose the treatments that these people would offer you by writing the letter for each treatment.

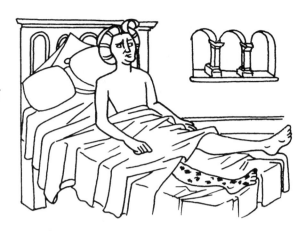

TREATMENTS

A Apply leeches to the leg
B Give you opium (a drug)
C Cut off your leg
D Give you holly-leaf tea
E Make you promise to go on a pilgrimage
F Consult a zodiac chart
G Look at the colour of your urine
H Throw holy water on your leg
I Hang a magpie's beak around your neck
J Give you eyedrops of rose water
K Chant a charm
L Cauterise the leg
M Make you gargle with acid
N Make you vomit
O Carry a pomander
P Open a vein
Q Pay money to the saints

A physician would

_____

_____

An apothecary would

_____

_____

A priest would

_____

A wise woman would

_____

A barber's surgeon would

_____

E Medicine

Look at page 68 in your textbook before studying the extract below.

> During the Crusades, there was a story told of an Arab doctor who was asked to heal a knight with an abscess on his leg and a woman with tuberculosis. The doctor began to treat them, putting a clean dressing on the knight's leg and prescribing a fresh diet for the woman.
>
> Suddenly a European doctor appeared. 'This man has no idea how to cure these people,' he said. Taking an axe, he cut off the leg of the knight, who died immediately. Declaring that the devil had got into the woman, he removed her brain and rubbed it with salt. She died instantly. 'I came away having learnt things about medicine that I never knew before,' commented the Arab doctor.

(From *Medieval Towns* by J D Clare, Bodley Head)

1 Which doctor would you have preferred to go to for treatment. Why?

_____

_____

_____

2 Why would the woman have believed the doctor when he said the devil had got into her?

_____

_____

_____

3 What modern treatments would have helped both patients?

_____

_____

_____

You will need

F Extension activity

Look at pages 70 and 71 in your textbook.

1 Complete the table below by writing the 'good' points and the 'bad' points of three inventions.

Invention	Good points of this invention	Bad points of this invention
Gunpowder		
Printing press		
Spinning-wheel		

2 I think _____ was the most important of the
three inventions because _____

_____

_____

3 a Consider all of the inventions you know of today. Which one
modern-day invention do you think is the most important?

_____

   b Why did you choose this? _____

_____

_____

You will need

A ## Basic skills: Prefixes

A prefix is placed at the beginning of a word to make it into another word with a similar meaning. For example:

Magna Carta   means   **Great Charter**

1   'Magn' is a prefix and comes from the Latin word 'magnus' which means 'great'.
    Look in a dictionary to find more words beginning with **'magn'** which have something to do with becoming or being great. List the words you find here.

    _____

    _____

2   A century is a hundred years. 'Centi' is a prefix and comes from the Latin word 'centum' which means 'hundred'.
    How many words can you find beginning with **'cent'** which have something to do with a hundred? List the words here.

    _____

    _____

3   'Prehistoric' means a period of time before history. The prefix 'pre' comes from Latin and means 'before'.
    How many words can you find beginning with **'pre'** which have something to do with before? List the words here.

    _____

    _____

4   The Magna Carta handed over (transferred) some power to the people. The prefix 'trans' comes from Latin and means 'across' or 'through'.
    How many words can you find beginning with **'trans'** which have something to do with across? List them here.

    _____

    _____

You will need

 B *Quick quiz*

Look at page 72 in your textbook.

Complete the sentences below by filling in the gaps.

1   King John's nicknames were _____

because _____

_____

and _____ because

_____

_____

2   During his reign, King John lost _____,

_____ and _____

to King Philip of France. John needed to raise taxes to pay for
an army to win back the land he had lost in France.

3   Relief money was _____

_____

4   King John raised scutage 11 times between 1199 and 1215.
Scutage was _____

_____

5   King John raised more money by tightening forest laws so that

_____

_____

 C ## Why was King John unpopular?

Look at pages 72 to 74 in your textbook.

This task will help you to make notes in order to answer the question: 'Why was King John unpopular?'

1 As you read the pages, look for information to fill in one section of the circle at a time. You will begin to build up your answer to the question in the middle of the circle.

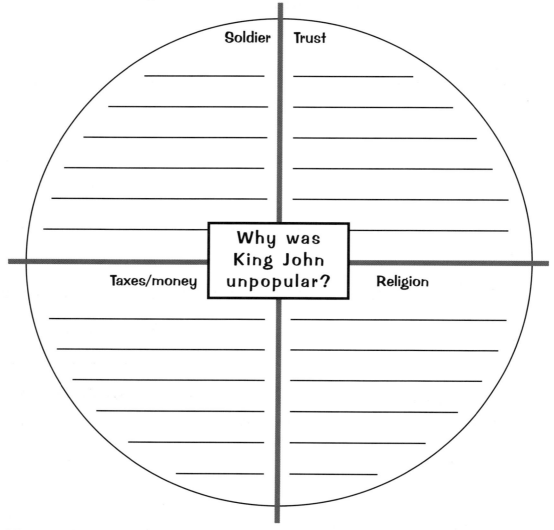

2 Now write your conclusion about King John:

a King John was unpopular because _____

_____

b My conclusion might be inaccurate because _____

_____

D 'Trouble with the Church'

Look at page 73 in your textbook.

1   Complete the sentence below by filling in the gaps.

The Pope wanted _____ _____ to be

Archbishop of Canterbury. King John refused. The Pope retaliated

and in 1208 placed England under an _____ and

_____ King John.

2   Interdict meant:

You could do this	You couldn't do this

3   How did King John retaliate?

a _____

b _____

4   Who won the argument between the Pope and King John?

_____ won because _____

_____

5   How did Archbishop Langton try to help the King in his
disagreement with the barons?

_____

_____

6   At first, did King John listen to the barons' complaints?

Yes ☐   No ☐

7   What happened next? _____

_____

E *Magna Carta extracts*

Look at pages 73 and 74 in your textbook.

Here are some extracts from the Magna Carta. Read each one and answer the same two questions for each extract.

1 What had happened in the past that the Magna Carta wanted to change?

2 Who would benefit from the change?

Clause 1: The English Church shall be free and have its rights withheld and its liberties unimpaired.	1 _____ 2 _____
Clause 4: The guardian of the land of such an heir who is under age shall not take from the land more than the reasonable revenues, customary dues and services, and that without destruction and waste of men or goods.	1 _____ 2 _____
Clause 12: No scutage or aid may be raised in our kingdom without general consent, unless to ransom ourself, to make our eldest son a knight and, once, to marry our eldest daughter.	1 _____ 2 _____
Clause 39: No free man shall be seized or imprisoned or stripped of his rights or possessions or outlawed or exiled, or deprived of his standing in any other way, nor will we use force against him, or send others to do so, except by the lawful judgement of his equals or by the law of the land.	1 _____ 2 _____
Clause 40: We will neither sell, delay nor deny right or justice to anyone.	1 _____ 2 _____
Clause 52: If anyone has been deprived of his lands, castles, liberties or rights without first hearing his pleas, we will restore them to him at once.	1 _____ 2 _____

F *Extension activity*

King John was one of English history's most controversial people. Here is what a number of historians have had to say about him.

Source A   By W L Warren, *King John*, 1961
▼

King John is one of the notoriously bad kings of English history, his name is forever associated with the humiliation inflicted on him at Runnymede in 1215. Yet there is a strong case for believing that he was not so much purposefully wicked as just unlucky.

Source B   By a 13th-century monk
▼

King John was drunk after dinner, and under the influence of the devil. He slew Arthur [his nephew] with his own hand.

Source C   By Roger of Wendover, a monk who lived at St Albans Abbey during the 13th century
▼

Foul as it is, hell itself is defiled by the fouler presence of John.

Source D   By R J Cootes, *The Middle Ages*, 1972
▼

He did not in fact hate the Church, but monks who wrote most of its Chronicles believed that a king who was excommunicated must be an evil monster.

Source E   From a 1960s school history book
▼

After losing Normandy he prowled restlessly round England staying only a few days in any place. No one knew where he would turn up next or what demand he would make when he came.

Source F   By R J Cootes, *The Middle Ages*, 1972
▼

John was always on the move, regularly visiting every corner of the country. On his travels he saw that laws were carried out, judged many disputes himself and kept a close watch on the work of the royal officials.

You will need

F *Extension activity (continued)*

1 Which of the sources A to F try to give a good impression of King John?

2 Does Source D agree with Sources B and C? Give reasons for your answer.

3 What do Sources E and F agree on?

4 What is the main difference between Sources E and F?

5 According to Source A, King John was just unlucky. Which other sources agree with this view?

6 Many of these sources were written at different times. How might this have an effect on what they have to say?

7 Although many monks hated John, and are biased in their opinions, why should we not dismiss the things that they say about him?

8 If you were writing a book about King John, are there any of these sources that you would <u>not</u> use? Give reasons for your answer.

You will need

Dictionary

A Basic skills: Using a dictionary

Even by the time of Edward I's Model Parliament, the barons and nobles had to swear to obey the king. The words and phrases at the bottom of the page indicate either **obedience** or **disobedience**. Write them in the correct column in the table below. Use a dictionary to help you.

Obedience	Disobedience

word of honour   refute   conform

swear allegiance   swear on the bible   confirm   disown

guarantee   renounce   defy   bow   agree   dissent

challenge   promise   revoke   loyalty

go back on your word   pledge   cross your heart

throw down the gauntlet   homage

You will need

B **Quick quiz**

Look at pages 76 and 77 in your textbook.

1 Parliament was made up of many people. Can you say who appointed these people to Parliament? Choose between

(King)   (Pope)   (Members of Parliament)

a Archbishop appointed by _____

b Barons appointed by _____

c Clerks appointed by _____

2 Add these labels to the picture below.

King   King's ministers   Clerks   Barons

Archbishop of Canterbury   Bishops   Judges

C | *How did Parliament develop?*

Look at pages 76 to 77 in your textbook.

1   The boxes below show how Parliament gradually developed from the time of William I until the time of Henry VII. Your task is to write them out in the correct order. The dates will help you.

> **King John (1199–1216) called a GREAT COUNCIL. This was made up of the barons and four knights from every county.**

> **William I (1066–1087) asked his great barons to give him advice. This was called the GREAT COUNCIL.**

> **Henry III (1216–1272) asked the knights from every county and the clergy to come to a meeting.**

> **Edward I (1272–1307) called a GREAT COUNCIL made up of lords, knights from every county and men from the main towns.**

> **Simon de Montfort defeated Henry III in 1264. He called a GREAT COUNCIL with barons, knights from each county and men from the towns.**

2   Answer these questions.

   a The first real Parliament was called by _____.

   b Edward I's Parliament was called the Model Parliament

      because _____.

   c Parliament has two parts. The House of Commons was a

      meeting place for _____ and

      _____. The House of Lords

      was a meeting place for the _____

      and the _____.

 Extension activity

The following is an extract taken from a record of the Good Parliament in 1376. At this time, apart from the important lords, bishops, barons and the king himself, there were also 280 other lesser nobles and people from towns and shires. The Parliament lasted 10 weeks.

> And on this the Lords and Commons deliberated concerning response, as the law requires. And at the same time at the end of speech, Sir John Knyvet, the Chancellor, commanded, on the King's behalf, the knights and burgesses and commons of the shires, on allegiance and under pain of forfeiture, that if there was anything redress or amend within the realm or if the realm was badly ruled, governed or treacherously counseled, by their good advice they will find remedy, in so far as they could, how the realm might be profitably governed to the honour of the King and its own profit. And so ended the first day. And the King went to his chamber, and the Lords and the Commons to their homes.

1 What does the expression, 'by their good advice they will find remedy' mean?

2 What sort of things did the King expect to be advised about?

3 Was this meeting held for a general discussion, or do you think the King wanted something specific from these people?

4 By asking for their advice, was the King automatically going to accept it?

5 How effective would a Parliament like this be for everyone to raise questions about the country?

A Basic skills: Nationalities

People born in Wales are called Welsh people. What are the people of the following countries called?

Look out for these endings:

       ese   **ians**   **ish**   **an**   **i**

COUNTRY	PEOPLE
Scotland	_____
France	_____
Spain	_____
Ireland	_____
Taiwan	_____
Russia	_____
Korea	_____
Japan	_____
Sweden	_____
Poland	_____
China	_____
Tibet	_____
Mexico	_____
Israel	_____
Argentina	_____

You will need

B **Quick quiz**

Look at pages 78 to 81 in your textbook.

<u>Underline</u> the correct answer from the words or phrases in brackets.

1   The border lands between England and Wales were known as the (Marches, badlands)

2   Conway, Rhuddlan and Harlech were Welsh (kings, castles).

3   The first English Prince of Wales became (Edward II, Charles, David).

4   David and Llewelyn were (brothers, cousins) who rebelled against the English.

5   David was (pardoned, 'hung, drawn and quartered') for rebelling.

6   Edward I chose (William Wallace, John Balliol) to be King of Scotland.

7   The Scots defeated the English at the Battle of (Stirling, Falkirk).

8   (William Wallace, Robert Bruce) was inspired by a spider.

9   The English were defeated by the Scots at the Battle of (Bannockburn, Ibrox).

10   Robert Bruce was finally accepted as King of Scotland in (1308, 1328).

You will need

C | *Beaumaris Castle*

Look at pages 78 and 79 in your textbook.

Beaumaris Castle was the last castle to be built on the instructions of Edward I. It was built to a concentric design, which means that the inner ward (guarded by high walls and towers) is surrounded by an outer ward (with a lower wall and smaller towers). The castle is symmetrical in its design: a tower or gateway on one side is matched by an identical tower or gateway on the other.

This plan needs to be completed. Finish the drawing and label it.

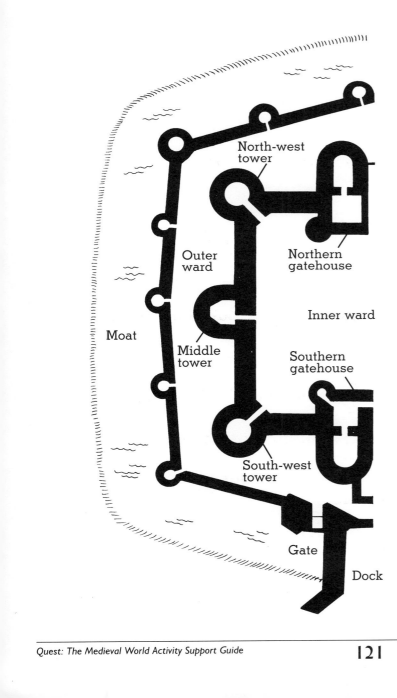

You will need

D *United kingdoms?*

Look at pages 78 to 81 in your textbook.

Study the map and answer the questions that follow.

The Kingdom of Scotland
Joined by land to England,
but separated by the use of:
- a different language
- different laws
- different customs
- different dress
- poorer farming land

The Kingdom of Wales
Joined by land to
England, but separated
by the use of:
- a different language
- different laws
- different customs
- different dress
- poorer farming land

The Kingdom of England
Rich, strong, large, powerful, good farming land.

1 Three countries share one island. Give four reasons why you think this might lead to warfare.

2 If a new leader ruled either Wales or Scotland, why might he want to attack England?

3 Explain why people living in the border areas would always be fearful of their neighbours.

 E *Scottish history*

Look at pages 80 and 81 in your textbook

All these years were significant in Scottish history. List the event for each year and decide what the consequence(s) were for Scotland. The first one has been done for you.

Year	Event(s)	Consequence for Scotland
1286	Alexander III died	Scotland lost a strong king
1290		
1292		
1296		
1297		
1298		
1304		
1305		
1306		
1314		
1328		
1328–1600s		

You will need

F Extension activity

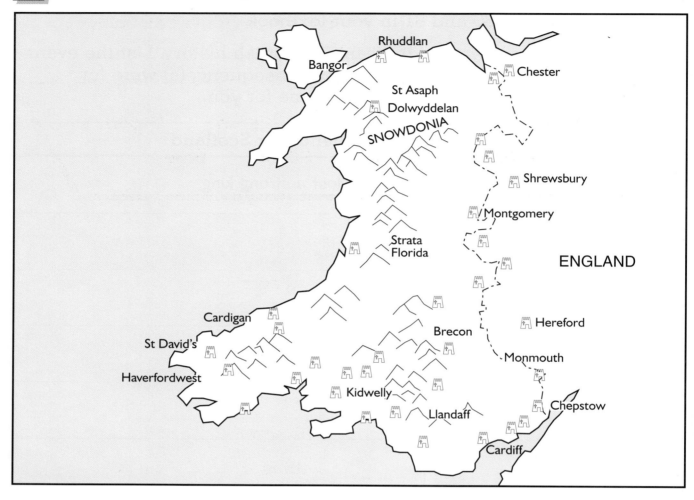

1 Using the same colour, shade all the castles on the map.
2 a How many castles are there?
  b How does this show that the English had trouble controlling the Welsh?
  c Why do you think there are not many castles in the mountainous areas of Wales?
3 Why would the English want to build a protective ring of castles around the Welsh mountains?
4 Why were many castles built on the eastern side of Wales?
5 Do you think the problems between the English and the Welsh would be solved effectively by building castles and by fighting?
6 Use page 79 in your textbook to find five things that Edward used to try to end the Welsh problem and to change things for the future.

 Basic skills: Colour words

Fill in the missing colours from the words in the box below.
Some of the words may be used more than once.

Black	**Yellow**	**Red**	**Scarlet**	**Green**
White	**Purple**	**Silver**	**Blue**	

_ _ _ _ _ Death

_ _ _ _ _ _ _ Fever

blood- _ _ _

_ _ _ _ _ sheep

_ _ _ _ _ _ Fever

_ _ _ _ _ with envy

_ _ _ _ _ with fear

_ _ _ _ _ _ with rage

_ _ _ _ _ _ with age

_ _ _ _ with cold

I'm in her _ _ _ _ _ books.

The business was a _ _ _ _ _ elephant.

It's a _ _ _ -letter day for the school.

_ _ _ _ blood of the aristocracy.

_ _ _ _ _ flag of surrender.

She gave me a _ _ _ _ _ look.

Clouds have a _ _ _ _ _ _ lining.

B **Quick quiz**

Look at pages 82 and 83 in your textbook.

1   Read page 82 and then name five symptoms of the Black Death. The first one has been done for you.

Buboes (boils)

2   People thought that the Black Death was caused by many different things. Read page 83 and then list five things that people thought caused the plague. The first one has been done for you.

a   <u>Foul vapours (smells) which came from volcanoes.</u>

b   _____

c   _____

d   _____

e   _____

C *Concoct a cure*

Look at pages 53, 69 and 85 in your textbook.

Concoct your own cure for the Black Death using ingredients found in medieval times.

1 Think about which ingredients you would choose, how you would make the cure (the 'method') and who you would give the medicine to. Some verbs to help you write the method are listed in the box at the bottom.

2 Give your recipe a name.

_____ cure for the plague

List of ingredients _____

_____

_____

Method _____

_____

_____

_____

This cure is suitable for _____

_____

_____

_____

Verbs to help you write the method

crush drain press boil simmer chop

dry twist say heat cool stir toast

mix stretch scrape pick

D A *bishop's* account

Look at pages 82 to 85 in your textbook.

Read this extract, which was written by William Edynton, Bishop of Winchester, in 1349:

> The plague kills more viciously than a two-edged sword. Nobody dares enter any town, castle or village where it has struck. Everyone flees them in terror as they would the lair of a savage beast. There is an awful silence in such places; no merry music, no laughter. They have become dens of terror, like a wilderness. Where the countryside was fertile, it has now become a barren desert, for there is nobody to plough the fields.

Bishop William was alive at the time of the Black Death. Find the words and phrases which express his feelings and write them here.

A feeling of fear

A feeling of sadness

A feeling of hopelessness

A feeling of fear for the future

You will need

E Symptoms

Look at page 82 in your textbook.

These symptoms of the Black Death have been listed in the wrong order. Cut out the boxes and stick them onto a clean sheet of paper in the correct order.

Small black spots and blue blotches would spread all over the body.

These would grow larger, sometimes as large as apples.

When people died, their bodies haemorrhaged (bled) under the skin which gave it a dark, mottled look.

Their breath turned foul and stinking.

Of all those that caught the disease, about two-thirds would be dead within a week.

First the victims would feel dizzy and weak.

Victims would sweat and have a fever.

They would have no energy.

Boils, called buboes, would appear under the arms and on the thighs.

The people vomited and spat blood.

F   A *monk's description*

Look at pages 82 to 85 in your textbook.

William Dene, a monk in Rochester, described the effect of the plague on one household:

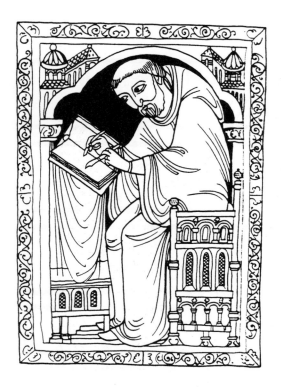

> The Bishop of Rochester didn't keep many servants or retainers. Yet he lost four priests, five gentlemen, ten serving men, seven young clerks, and six pages, so that not a soul remained to serve him in any post. During the epidemic, many chaplains and paid clerics would serve only if they were paid excessive salaries... Priests hurried off to places where they could get more money than in their own benefices [parishes]... There was also so great a shortage of labourers and workmen of every kind in those days that more than a third of the land over the whole kingdom lay uncultivated.

1   How many people died altogether in the Bishop of Rochester's house?

2   How can we tell that the Bishop of Rochester survived the plague? (Clue: Past tense)

3   Historians know more details about the numbers of monks and clergy who died during the plague than other sections of the population. Why is this? (Clue: Look at the picture above)

4   What special services could a priest offer that might make him more money than usual?

5   If there were fewer workers on the land, what might they hope to expect?

6   Why was there a great danger of famine and starvation at this time?

You will need
Dictionary

Study these pictures carefully and then answer the questions on the next page.

Picture A

Picture B

You will need

G *Extension activity (continued)*

1 Pictures A and B are copies of contemporary illustrations. Use a dictionary to find out the meaning of the word 'contemporary' and write it here.

_____

2 The two pictures give slightly different interpretations of the Black Death.

   a Which picture do you think has the greatest impact on the audience? Why do you think this is?

   _____

   _____

   b Both pictures portray death in different ways. What are the main differences?

   _____

   _____

   c How do the two main figures in both pictures cause the death of their victims?

   Picture A: _____

   Picture B: _____

   d In Picture B, why is death sometimes called the Grim Reaper?

   _____

   _____

   e Explain why the eyes in the 'Mors' (Latin for 'death') figure in Picture A are covered by a hood.

   _____

   _____

A *Basic skills: Possessive apostrophes*

In this worksheet you will learn about apostrophes to show possession (belonging).

- The Revolt belonging to one peasant ➠ The Peasant's Revolt
  (Rule: In singular words, write the apostrophe before the s)

- The Revolt belonging to two or more peasants ➠ The Peasants' Revolt
  (Rule: In plural words, put the apostrophe after the s)

1 Add the apostrophes in these statements.

   a The sons belonging to the king ➠ The kings sons

   b William was a friend of Harold ➠ Harolds friend was William

   c The weapons belonging to the footsoldiers ➠ The footsoldiers weapons

   d The shops belonging to William ➠ Williams ships

   e The land belonging to the barons ➠ The barons land

   f The oxen belonging to the peasants ➠ The peasants oxen

   g The speech belonging to the Pope ➠ The Popes speech

2 Are these singular or plural? Write S or P for each. The first one has been done for you.

   a The knights' estates   (P)

   b The baron's armour   ◯

   c People's lives   ◯

   d Caxton's books   ◯

   e King Henry's son   ◯

   f Richard's promises   ◯

   g Peasants' Revolt   ◯

   h The villeins' labour services   ◯

   i The Sheriff of Essex's house   ◯

   j The rebels' death   ◯

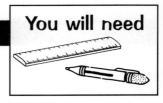

You will need

B Quick quiz

Look at pages 86 to 89 in your textbook.

<u>Underline</u> the correct answer from the words or phrases in brackets.

1   The peasants rebelled after a (poll tax, ship tax) was made law.

2   The peasants did not want to pay taxes for a war against (Spain, France).

3   The peasants' army marched to (London, Canterbury).

4   The leader of the peasants' rebellion was (Wat Tyler, King Richard).

5   John Ball was a (soldier, priest).

6   John Ball had been imprisoned earlier for (not paying taxes, plotting an uprising).

7   The King found sanctuary from the peasants by going to (the Tower of London, Windsor Castle).

8   The King met Wat Tyler at (World's End, Mile End).

9   Wat Tyler demanded that a lord had to pay (wages, taxes) to his peasants in return for working on the land.

10   The ministers who organised the poll tax were (pardoned, executed) by the rebels.

11   Wat Tyler was killed by (the Mayor of London, a squire).

12   The King (kept, did not keep) the promises that he had made to the peasants.

13   The ringleaders of the Revolt were (pardoned, executed) by the King's army.

14   The Peasants' Revolt is an important event in (English, French) history.

C Pictures of the Revolt

Look at pages 86 to 89 in your textbook.

Study these pictures before answering the questions on the second sheet.

▲
Picture A
The peasants had a hard life. They got very little pay.

▲
Picture B
Many peasants died from the Black Death.

◄ **Picture C**
There was a shortage of peasants to work on the land. The peasants were happy. The shortage forced the lords to pay better wages to work for them.

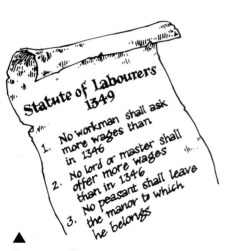

▲
Picture D
The government did not like this. They were worried that the peasants would ask for more and more. Parliament passed a law called the Statute of Labourers.

▲
Picture E
The Statute of Labourers stopped the peasants getting better pay. The peasants got angry. They knew they were stronger now because of the Black Death. They rebelled against the king.

C Pictures of the Revolt (continued)

Picture A

This man is called a p_____.

He looks very s_____.

He gets paid very little for his w_____.

Picture B

Many peasants died from the B_____ D_____.

Picture C

The men getting money are called p_____.

The peasants look h_____.

There is a s_____ of peasants to work on the land.

The Black Death means they can get h_____ wages.

Picture D

Parliament passed a law called the Statute of L_____.

This law stopped the peasants getting h_____ wages.

This law stopped the peasants l_____ their villages.

Picture E

These men are called p_____.

They look very a_____.

They have r_____ against the king.

 D **Historical chain**

Look at pages 86 to 89 in your textbook.

Using any of the events of the Peasants' Revolt, fill in the main links in the chain below showing how one event caused another event to happen. You can choose any six events, but they must have a proper link. In historical terms this is called **causation**.

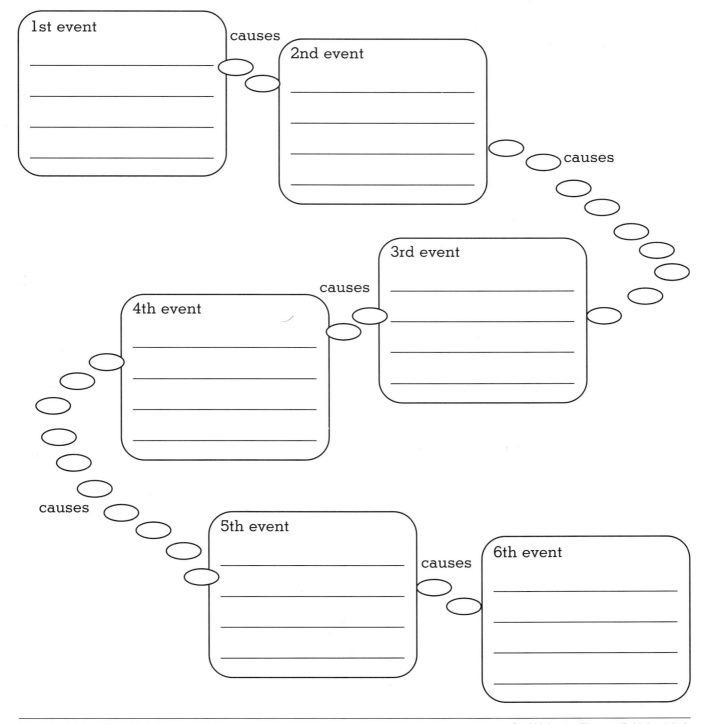

1st event

causes

2nd event

causes

3rd event

causes

4th event

causes

5th event

causes

6th event

 A *law case*

Look at pages 86 to 89 in your textbook.

Read this extract from a law case of 1381 and answer the questions in sentences.

> LONDON. John Lovell, knight, was attached to answer Walter Ethalf in a plea why he assaulted the said Walter at London by force of arms and beat, wounded and imprisoned him, ill-treated him and committed other enormities against him.
>
> John in his own person comes and says that the said Walter ought not to be answered because he says that the same Walter is his villein as of his manor of Southmere in Norfolk and that he and his ancestors, lords of the manor aforsaid have been seised [owners] of the said Walter and his ancestors as of their villeins belonging to the manor from time out of mind...

1 What had happened in England at this time to force Walter to leave his village?

2 Why would the knight, John Lovell, want Walter to return?

3 What argument does John Lovell use to defend himself?

4 How do you think lords of the manor like John Lovell regarded their villeins at this time in history?

5 How could this court case reflect the desperate shortage of labour there was at this time?

6 This extract is a **primary source of evidence**. This means that it really exists and comes from the 14th century. Why do you think historians like to work with this sort of evidence?

F Extension activity

Read the following sources and answer the questions.

Source A By Professor K Feiling, writing in 1950
▼

Castles like Rochester were tamely surrendered, boroughs like Canterbury took oaths from the 'commons' for ten days. Council [the King's Council], Tower garrison [the troops in the Tower of London] and nobles had done nothing.

Source B By Professor V H H Green in 1955
▼

Since royal armies were still feudal in composition, there was no standing force [army] able to take the offensive. The magnates [chief lords and barons] like the government required time to rally the loyal forces to deal with the situation.

Source C From Parliament, November 1381, quoted by Professor V H H Green
▼

Prelates, lords temporal, knights, citizens and burgesses responded with one voice that the repealing of the charters was well done. No promise could be made without their consent and they would never consent even to save themselves from sudden death.

Source D Written in 1972 by R J Cootes
▼

Once the rebels were safely dispersed, the King and his Council broke all promises made at Mile End and Smithfield. At Waltham the King told a gathering of peasants, 'Villeins you were and villeins you shall remain.'

1 Read Source A. How can we tell that Professor Feiling blames the government for letting things get out of hand?
2 In Source B how does Professor Green explain why it took so long for the government to react to the Revolt?
3 Do you think Source A or B is correct in giving reasons for the Revolt, or do you think both have elements of truth in them?
4 What do Sources A and B agree on?
5 How does Source C explain why the King could never keep the promises made to the peasants?
6 How does Source D give the impression that the King was to blame for breaking the promises he had made?
7 Both Sources C and D use quotations from that time. Which one do you think gives the best information about what happened after the Revolt?
8 Which sources would the peasants approve of and why?
9 Which sources would the barons approve of and why?

A Basic skills: Nouns

Some people in towns enjoyed great wealth. Some people experienced poverty and illness. The words 'wealth', 'poverty' and 'illness' are abstract nouns. These are nouns that cannot actually be seen, heard, smelt, felt or tasted.
Sort out these nouns and write each one in the correct column. The first ones have been done for you.

Common nouns	Proper nouns	Collective nouns	Abstract nouns
soldier	January	herd	fear

~~soldier~~   ~~January~~   ~~herd~~   ~~fear~~   power   shield
freedom   state   Scotland   swarm   pack
wine   army   sheaf   Gascony
fleet   pair   flock   cavalry   death
King Edward   terror   starvation   archer   coffin
courage   treachery   team

You will need

B Quick quiz

Look at page 92 in your textbook.

Consider whether these statements are true or false, or if there is not enough evidence to decide.

Fill in the boxes with your answers.

True	False	Not enough evidence
✓	✗	?

1 Animals were slaughtered by butchers in the street.

2 People enjoyed living in towns.

3 People would empty chamberpots straight onto the street.

4 Rats roamed the streets spreading disease.

5 The streets were cleaned daily.

6 The streets became open sewers.

7 Most of the people who lived in London were wealthy.

8 The population of London was greater than all other towns at that time.

9 Everyone would be expected to help with the annual harvest.

10 Street cleaners were poorly paid in medieval times.

 C *Merchant guilds*

Look at page 93 in your textbook.

Each merchant guild had its own badge which was known as its 'coat of arms'. The coat of arms was generally very detailed and gave many clues in its design to show which guild it belonged to.

Design a modern 'coat of arms' or badge for the following guilds. (Note that some of them do not *really* exist.)

Guild of shoemakers

Guild of leatherworkers

Guild of computer programmers

Guild of beauticians

Guild of car mechanics

D Imports

Look at page 95 in your textbook.

Fill in 'exports from' and 'imports to' England in the boxes below.

Imports

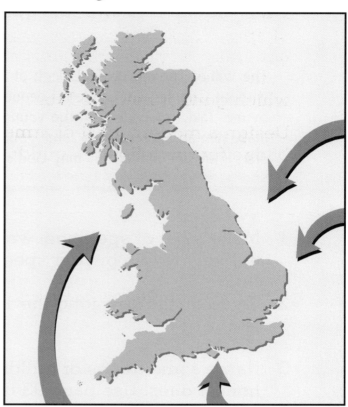

Exports

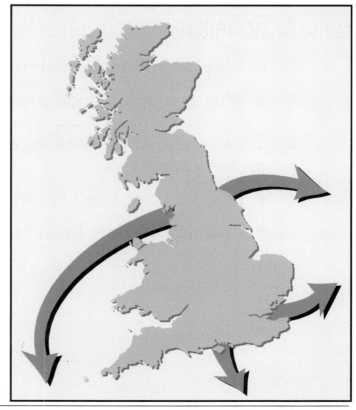

 Guilds and apprentices

Look at page 93 in your textbook.

Read this primary source, an extract from a will dated March 22, 1407, and then answer the questions.

> The Will of Thomas de Tyldeslegh of Eccles, Lancaster, and of St Giles without Cripplegate, London: I bequeath to John Boys, otherwise called by me 'Jakke of Tyldeslegh tho younge', one hundred shillings silver to make him an apprentice in some good and honest trade and in no evil one. If anyone hinder this may God's curse be upon him.

1   Make a list of spellings, words and phrases that you would be unlikely to use in your speech and writing today.

2   Try to guess how long the 100 silver shillings was meant to last.

3   Name some trades or guilds that you think would be good and honest ones. Use page 93 in your textbook to help you.

4   Explain in your own words the meaning of the last sentence.

5   a Why do you think historians like to study wills like this?

    b Why is a will a good primary source?

6   Choose one of these titles and write a couple of paragraphs giving your views.

    ● I would have liked to have been an apprentice because...

    ● I would not have liked to have been an apprentice because...

 Extension activity

Read these two sources about the merchant guilds and then answer the questions.

Source A Written in 1340

The Gild Merchant of Coventry buries its members at the Gild expense in need. In unmerited poverty it helps members get started in trade and gives assistance in sickness. It maintains 31 brothers and sisters who cannot work at a yearly cost of £35 3/-.

Source B Written in 1369

The Gild of St George the Martyr, in the Charnel House next to St Nicholas Church, Great Yarmouth finds for its members in poverty 7½d per week, a tunic with a hood and other clothing, and also burial at the Gild's expense in need.

1 How do these sources show how useful it was to be part of a large and helpful organisation?

2 Why do you think Source A calls its members brothers and sisters?

3 Both sources mention burial as one of the services it offers to members. Why do you think this service was included by the guilds?

4 List the things in Sources A and B that guilds do to help their members. Try to place similar things alongside each other. For example:

Source A	Source B
Gives money: £35 3/- a year	Gives money: 7½d a week

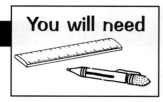

You will need

 A *Basic skills: Homophones*

A homophone is a word with the same sound as another word but with a different meaning and spelling to that other word. For example, **to** and **two**.

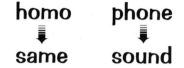

homo → same
phone → sound

1 The words in brackets below sound the same. Underline the correct spelling of the word to complete these sentences.

  a The English (nights, knights) fought bravely.

  b The English had to (sale, sail) over the English Channel to reach France.

  c Many of the soldiers wanted (peace, piece).

  d During the Battle you could (hear, here) the wounded soldiers crying in agony.

  e The soldiers did not want to (die, dye).

  f The King wanted to see his (sun, son) again.

  g The sound of the (canons, cannons) grew louder.

  h The English sent scouts to see (where, wear) the French were.

  i The French (caught, court) the English at Crécy.

  j The English (new, knew) they could win the battle.

2 Make up five new sentences like those above containing your own homophones.

_____

_____

_____

_____

_____

_____

_____

You will need

B *Quick quiz*

Look at page 99 in your textbook.

1   In the picture above, find and label the following:
    a English standard (flag).   **d** Foot soldiers.
    b French standard (flag).   **e** Longbow.
    c Cavalry.   **f** Crossbow

2   Fill in the gaps in the following paragraph, using the words in
    the box at the bottom.

In August _____, after a raid in Normandy, the French army

caught up with Edward at _____. Edward's army had about

12,000 men. King _____ army had about 24,000 men.

Edward chose a good _____ position and his longbowmen

fired showers of _____. Philip's archers used _____.

These fired iron-tipped bolts released by a trigger. The drawback

with these was that they took too long to _____ in battle

and they could not shoot as far as the _____. As the French

knights charged, English arrows brought them crashing to the

ground. There they were _____ to death by horses or

_____ by their own armour.

re-load	Philip's	trampled	1346	Crécy
suffocated	defensive	longbow	arrows	crossbows

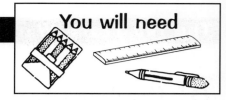

You will need

C | *The longbow*

Look at page 98 in your textbook.

1 Complete this picture of a longbowman and label it.

2 Here is a selection of arrow-heads used at the time. Choose one and draw it on the end of the arrow.

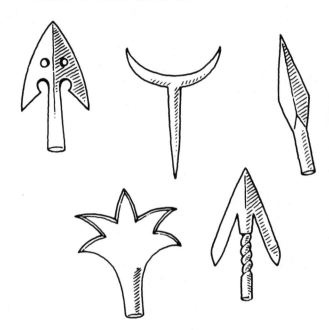

3 Describe the archer and his bow and arrow. Say why the longbow was such an effective weapon.

_____

_____

_____

_____

_____

_____

_____

D The Battle of Agincourt

This diagram shows what penetrative power the English longbow possessed. Look at the diagram and answer the questions below.

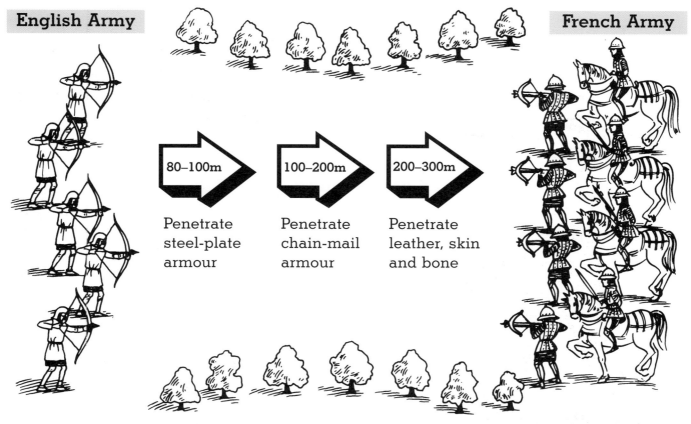

English Army

French Army

80–100m Penetrate steel-plate armour

100–200m Penetrate chain-mail armour

200–300m Penetrate leather, skin and bone

1 At what range could the English inflict the first casualties on the enemy?

2 Why would the archers target the horses?

3 An English longbowman could fire six arrows per minute. There were at least 5,000 archers at Agincourt. How many arrows could be fired at the French each minute?

4 A Frenchman at Agincourt said, 'The arrows fell like hail.' Using your answer to question 3, explain what he meant.

5 Explain why the French could not attack the sides of the English army at Agincourt.

6 Heavy rain had made the battlefield at Agincourt extremely muddy. How would this help the English and hinder the French?

7 The closer they got to the English longbowmen, the more dangerous it would be for the French knights. Explain why.

You will need

E *War grid*

Look at pages 97 to 104 in your textbook.

Study the grid of the 100 Years' War on the next page.

1 Fill in the missing dates and details. Each square stands for one year.

2 Colour in **red** any event, battle, siege, raid or time when the English won or were in control.

3 Colour in **yellow** any event, battle, siege, raid or time when the French won or were in control.

4 Colour in **blue** the squares when there was peace or a peace treaty.

5 Colour in **green** the squares when there was a break in fighting.

6 **a** How many 'fighting' squares have been coloured in?

   b How many 'peace' and 'break in fighting' squares have been coloured in?

7 Compare your answers in question 6. Is it correct to call this the 100 Years' War? Explain your answer.

You will need

E | War grid (continued)

1340 Battle of						1346 Battle of	1347	1348	1349
1350					1355	1356 Battle of			
1360 Treaty of									1369
1370	1371						1377		
1380									
1390						1396			
1400									
1410			1413		1415 Battle of				
1420 Treaty of		1422 Death of						1428 Siege of	
1430	1431 Death of				1435 English lose				
1440									
1450			1453						

 F *Extension activity*

1 During the 100 Years' War, the Battle of Crécy, the Battle of Poitiers and the Battle of Agincourt were all English victories. A French noble who fought the English at this time said, 'The French had forgotten nothing and remembered nothing.' What do you think he meant by this?

2 Look at this diagram. It is called a 'herce' and was used by the English during battles.

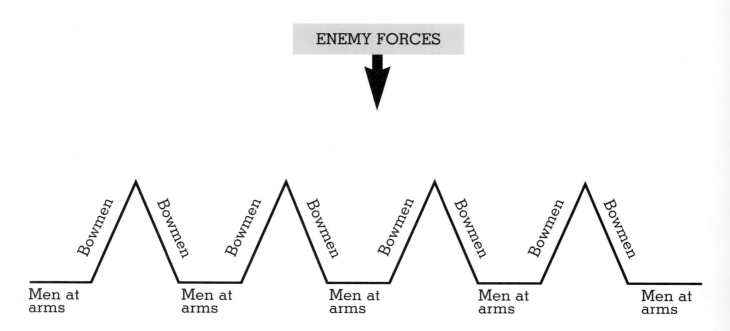

a Think of three reasons why this formation might be better than using a single or double straight line of troops.

b A weakness of this formation is the vulnerability of the edges. How would you solve this weakness?

3 From your knowledge of the battles, would you say it was English skill or French incompetence that caused the English victories? You might decide that other factors, such as the weather, resulted in the victories. Give reasons for your opinions.

A Basic skills: Sentences

Put a ✓ in the box for each statement if you think it is a proper sentence. Put a ✗ if it is not.

1   That was a civil war.

2   The House of Lancaster and the House of York.

3   The red rose

4   Not all of the time!

5   The wars were confusing because there were plots and counter-plots.

6   there were executions and murders.

7   Richard of York

8   What are civil wars?

9   Edward V, twelve years old.

10   richard his uncle arrested his escort

11   By the end of June

12   The princes had been seen playing in the garden.

13   Did Richard really order the murder of the two innocent princes?

14   Their mother, accused of witchcraft

15   edward was put in the Tower of London.

You will need

B Quick quiz

Look at pages 105 and 110 in your textbook.

Can you identify these kings from the Wars of the Roses?
For each king:

1 Fill in his name;
2 Write the name of the 'house' he belonged to;
3 Colour in the rose, or leave it white;
4 Fill in the born and died dates.

	House of		Born
	_____		Died _____
	House of _____		Born Died _____
	House of _____		Born Died _____
	House of _____		Born Died _____
	House of _____		Born Died _____
	House of _____		Born Died _____
	House of _____		Born Died _____

You will need

C Timeline

Look at page 105 in your textbook.

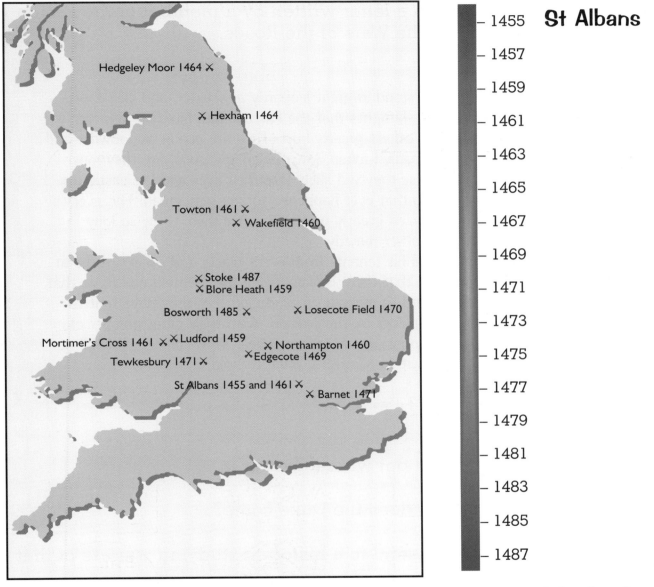

– 1455	**St Albans**
– 1457	
– 1459	
– 1461	
– 1463	
– 1465	
– 1467	
– 1469	
– 1471	
– 1473	
– 1475	
– 1477	
– 1479	
– 1481	
– 1483	
– 1485	
– 1487	

Map labels: Hedgeley Moor 1464, Hexham 1464, Towton 1461, Wakefield 1460, Stoke 1487, Blore Heath 1459, Bosworth 1485, Losecote Field 1470, Mortimer's Cross 1461, Ludford 1459, Northampton 1460, Tewkesbury 1471, Edgecote 1469, St Albans 1455 and 1461, Barnet 1471

1   Complete the timeline by writing in the names of the battles from the map.

2   'Because there were only _____ battles over _____ years, I think it is wrong to call this period the "Wars of the Roses". It should be called the "War of the Roses".' Do you agree or disagree with this statement? Give a reason for your answer. .

3   Why do historians call this period the Wars of the Roses?

You will need

D A *family extract*

Look at page 105 in your textbook.

Read this extract from a letter written by a member of the Paston family at the time of the Wars of the Roses.

> Your brother and his men stand in great jeopardy at Caister, and lack food, and Daubeney and Berney [knights that the Pastons had hired to fight for them] be dead, and many others greatly hurt. They are out of gunpowder and arrows, and the castle is badly broken down by enemy guns. So, they must have speedy help, otherwise they will likely lose their lives and the castle, to the greatest shame to you that ever happened to any gentleman. For, every man in the country is amazed greatly that you suffer them to be so long in jeopardy without help or other remedy.
>
> The Duke has sent for all his tenants from every place, and others, to be at Caister on Thursday next, that there is likely to be the greatest multitude that came there yet. They intend to make a great assault. For they have sent to Lynn for guns, and other places by the seaside. With their great number of guns, shot and other weapons, no man dare appear in the place... It shall not lie in the power of those within [Caister Castle] to hold it.

1 Use an atlas to find out where Caister is.

2 From which county does the Duke come?

3 Why is this letter useful to a historian studying warfare of that period in history?

4 Are there any words or phrases that might suggest that the writer is exaggerating the situation?

5 Do you think the letter was written by a man or a woman? Explain why.

6 Why might a modern historian be wary of accepting this letter as a wholly accurate description of this event?

 Extension activity

Study the map and the three other sources before answering the questions.

Source A

X Battle sites

▨ The area where the Paston family lived

0   100 km

Source B From a letter written in 1462 by Margaret Paston to her husband, John, who was in London at the time. She is describing a local incident during the Wars of the Roses.

The people in this part of the world are beginning to grow wild. Indeed, men are very afraid here of a rising of the common people. God in His holy mercy give grace that a good government is soon set up in these parts, because I never heard of so much robbery and manslaughter here as there has been recently.

Source C From a school textbook published in 1930

The nobles threw themselves eagerly into the struggle, and many battles were fought in different parts of England. It was a dreary war, for everybody was fighting for his own reasons and men changed sides shamelessly when it suited them.
   All men rejoiced when the Wars of the Roses were over, for indeed it was an unhappy, lawless time.

Source D From a book about the Wars of the Roses, published in 1976

For the ordinary Englishman the effects of civil war were much less than for the dukes, barons and earls. English life in general was very little affected by 30 years of war. There was very little devastation, little pillaging and plundering. There was no general collapse of law and order.

1 Does Source A give you the impression that the whole of England was affected by the Wars of the Roses?

2 Give two reasons why you think Source B might be a reliable source of information and two reasons why it might not be reliable.

3 What do Sources C and D agree and disagree about?

You will need

A Basic skills: Paragraphs

A paragraph is a group of sentences linked by the same idea or theme. It can be just one sentence.

These paragraphs about the Princes in the Tower have been jumbled up. Cut them out and stick them in the right order. Use page 106 in your textbook to help you.

He was escorted by his mother's relations. Richard, his uncle, stopped the prince and arrested his escort. The escort was murdered and Edward was put in the Tower of London. He was joined by his younger brother, Richard, after threats about his safety were made to their mother, Queen Elizabeth.

By the end of June, Parliament had been persuaded to accept a document which asked that Richard should be made King. Richard was crowned on July 6, 1483.

Their uncle, Richard, accused their mother of witchcraft. He said that Edward and Richard were illegitimate because their father, Edward IV, had made a marriage contract with someone else before marrying Elizabeth.

The princes had been seen playing in the garden of the Tower during summer, but after that they were never seen again.

Edward V was only 12 years old when he travelled to London to prepare for his coronation.

B Quick quiz

Look at pages 108 to 110 in your textbook.

1   How many kings between 1004 and 1509 were buried at Westminster Abbey?

2   Why have the birth dates of Edward and Harold II got question marks beside them?

3   Who was the uncrowned king?

4   Who was the youngest king at the age of succession?

5   a Which king had the most children?

    b How many children did he have?

6   Why did kings want children?

7   How many kings died in France?

8   Which king reigned for the shortest time?

9   Which king reigned for the longest time?

10 Which king was named 'Crookback' and why?

11 Which kings died of dysentery?

12 Whose heart was not buried with the rest of his body?

13 How many English cathedrals are mentioned?

14 How many English abbeys are mentioned?

15 Which king lived the longest?

C Extension activity

Look at pages 108 to 110 in your textbook.

Choose one king and write several paragraphs about him.

a You should include the following details:

> **name   date of birth   date of succession
> family details   age at death   when he died
> what he died of   where he was buried**

b To make your account more interesting, find out more from your textbook about the king you have chosen and include the findings in your writing.

The following paragraph 'starters' may be useful:

I have chosen King _____ to write about.

I discovered that...

I also learnt that...

I thought it was interesting that...

As you can see...

Finally...